The Life Beyond the Veil
Volume 2

The Highlands of Heaven

The Life Beyond the Veil series consists of five volumes:

The Lowlands of Heaven
The Highlands of Heaven
The Ministry of Heaven
The Battilions of Heaven
The Outlands of Heaven

Spirit Messages received and set down by the Rev. George Vale Owen. (1860-1931) Vicar of Orford, Lancashire, England.

ISBN: **978-1-329-80574-3**

The Life Beyond the Veil Volume 2

The Highlands of Heaven

LONDON

COPYRIGHT April 1920

PRINTED IN THE UNITED KINGDOM.

    This volume was printed in April 1920, April 1926, April 1929, April 1946, Jan 1948 and April 1950. It was also printed in the U.S.A.
    This new print version was created by Geoff Cutler in January 2016 and no copyright is claimed in this publication. This edition contains the preface from both the first 1920 edition and the revised 1949 edition, as I found that there is slightly different information contained in each. Obviously the reader can simply skip one of these if they have little interest in the background of Rev. George Vale Owen. In this volume I have removed some of the archaic language that exists in the original text and attempted to keep the volume appropriate for the modern reader, without totally altering the character of the book. I have also added numerous footnotes.

THE REV. G. VALE OWEN
VICAR OF ORFORD, LANCS.,
1908-1922

The Rev. George Vale Owen, Vicar of Orford from 1908 to 1922.

Highlands of Heaven

The Church of St. Margaret and All Hallows, Orford, Warrington, Lancashire, England.

Table of Contents

Foreword (1946) ix

An Appreciation xi
    By Lord Northcliffe...xi

Preface (1925) xiii
    The Personality of Mr. Vale Owen. xiv
    Mr. Vale Owen's World-Wide Correspondence. xvi
    General Notes how the Messages Came xvii
    About Zabdiel who Communicated. xviii
    A Message from Zabdiel. xx
    The Reality of Zabdiel. xxi
    Angelic Love xxiii

Preface (1946) xxvii
    How The Messages Came xxviii

Introduction xxix
    By Sir Arthur Conan Doyle xxix

Chapter 1 1
    Divine Love. 4
    Human Blindness. 5
    Evil and Good. 7
    Evolution. 8
    Unity in Diversity. 11

Chapter 2 15
    Men and Angels 15
    Degrees of Light in the Spheres. 15
    Geometrical Astronomy. 18

Highlands of Heaven

    The Orbit of Human Life. 19

    Angel Visitants to Earth. 21

    The Wrestling of Jacob. 22

    The Power of a Name. 23

    Courage in Thinking. 25

    The Divinity of the Christ. 26

    Love and its Opposite. 28

    "Now we see Through a Glass Darkly." 30

    Zabdiel's Heavenly Home. 30

Chapter 3 33

    The Earthly and the Heavenly 33

    Recurring Science. 33

    Tales of Faerie and Magic. 34

    The Passing of Materialism. 35

The Inter-Relation of the Spheres. 36

    Purified by Suffering. 38

    The Origin of Species. 41

    Man's Place in the Universe. 42

Chapter 4 45

    Earth the Vestibule of Heaven 45

    Inspiration. 45

    Like Attracts Like. 48

    The Squire and his Wife. 49

    Our Spiritual Status. 52

    The Man who Thought he Knew. 53

    The Penalty of Spiritual Blindness. 56

Chapter 5 61

    The Science of the Heavens 61

    Transmission of Spiritual Power. 61

    The Relation of Spirit to Matter 62

    Consider the Heavens. 64

    The Web of Light. 65

    Spiritual Reality. 67

    The Reality of Heaven. 68

    The City by the Lake 69

    Old Comrades Meet. 73

    The Temple and its Sanctuary. 74

Chapter 6 77

    The Summerland of God 77

    "Teach me Thy Way." 77

    The Glade of the Statue. 80

    Flora of the Tenth Sphere. 81

    The Sanctuary of Festivals. 81

    A Heavenly Vista. 83

    The Meeting at the Valley of the Peaks. 84

    The Meeting with Harolen. 88

    To the Gate of the Sea. 90

    Laus Deo. 91

    The Altar on the Raft. 92

    "One Lord, One Faith." 94

    A Heavenly Transfiguration. 97

    The Son of Man 98

Chapter 7 101

- The Highlands of Heaven 101
- At the Children's Home. 101
- A Lesson in Creative Faith. 102
- At the Village of Bepel. 105
- Joy and Sorrow of the Angels. 107
- Into the Highlands. 108
- The Highland Watch-Tower. 109
- How Messages are Received There. 110
- An Horizon of Glory. 112
- Walls of Light. 114
- Motherhood Enthroned. 114
- The Crimson Glory of the Christ 116
- A Colony with a Problem. 118

Chapter 8 121

- Come Ye Blessed and Inherit. 121
- Zabdiel's Mission to the Fifth Sphere. 121
- The Capital City of Sphere Five. 122
- Zabdiel's Test of the Faithful Women. 125
- The Constitution of Sphere Five. 129
- Into the Sixth Sphere. 130
- The Initiation in the Sanctuary. 131
- Back in the Tenth Sphere. 133
- The Temple of the Holy Mount. 134
- The King of Kings. 135
- The Power and the Glory. 137

  Zabdiel's Farewell 140

Recommended Reading 141

  The Padgett Messages. 141

  The Judas Messages. 142

  Trilogy by Robert James Lees. 142

  Anthony Borgia and Monsignor Robert Hugh Benson. 142

  Other Books. 143

Foreword (1946)

The Greater World Association have undertaken to reprint the four volumes comprising the illuminating Scripts received through the mediumship of the Rev. G. Vale Owen. It has been a great loss to the Movement that these books have been out of print for so long, for it is generally agreed that no other communications from Spirit Realms have had such a wide appeal to the world at large. This is due partly, we know, to the extensive publicity given to them by that great newspaper Proprietor, Lord Northcliffe, who, ignoring general prejudice and cynicism regarding the possibility of such communications, published them serially in The WEEKLY DESPATCH in 1920-21, and spent a great deal of money in announcing their appearance.

It is natural to ask: "How were these Spirit Messages received?" The answer is given by Vale Owen himself in the first book of the series. The Lowlands of Heaven.

Then comes the next question: "What was this clergyman like?" Those who did not meet Vale Owen might well picture a dreamer, a man separated from the usual things of daily life—a saint or an ascetic. But although all who knew Vale Owen personally had no doubt about his spirituality, they would not agree that he was a man who "lived in the clouds"; rather he was one who needed human love and the gladness of physical life.

We are very grateful, therefore, to the Rev. G. Eustace Owen for giving us a few details about his father which shows that he was a practical man with a sense of humour and a great tolerance for the weakness of others, which means that he was a very good companion as well as a good Christian. The Rev. Eustace Owen writes:

"In his book WITH NORTHCLIFFE IN FLEET STREET, J. A. Hammerton alludes to the Rev. Vale Owen as 'that typical visionary of the half-Christian, half-spiritualist sort.' That view is held by many people who knew him through his writings; but it is not a true portrait. My father was a visionary without being a crank. While having a clear view of life's spiritual basis, he was most practical and methodical in all his ways.

"I remember how gently he dealt with others, how broad-minded he was in argument, his tolerance of opponents, and how he endured persecution with immense patience. Many an opponent's sword was blunted by his understanding of the one who wielded it! Yet he could be severe when necessary. Cruelty in any form roused his indignation. To bullies and schemers he became a very Elijah!

"I have never known anyone more direct in thought and words, or one who so detested shams. Beneath his graciousness lay the hardness of a good soldier of the Cross, so that he bore scorn and persecution without wavering. Quietness sometimes conceals a rare courage.

"In the book HE LAUGHED IN FLEET STREET, Bernard Falk describes a meeting between Lord Northcliffe and my father, in 'The Times' office, when the former asked him to accept £1,000 for publishing extracts from the Script in the 'Weekly Despatch.'

"He continues:

'Vale Owen shook his head. For this part of his writings, he said, he could not take any money. He had been well paid by the publicity given him, and by being able to carry out the sacred duty of placing his revelations before the world. Knowing well Vale Owen's poverty I was genuinely sorry to hear him refuse payment, but he was not to be dissuaded. .

The Rev. G. Eustace Owen adds :

"All our family are pleased that the Script is not to be allowed to remain in oblivion. The rising generation particularly need the comfort and illumination of its message. We are all so glad that 'The Greater World' have so keenly and so boldly taken up this re-publication. May their confidence be justified and their labours blessed!"

An Appreciation

By Lord Northcliffe[1]

I have not had an opportunity of reading the whole of The Life Beyond the Veil, but among the passages I have perused are many of great beauty.

It seems to me that the personality of the Rev. G. Vale Owen is a matter of deep importance and to be considered in connection with these very remarkable documents. During the brief interview that I had with him I felt that I was in the presence of a man of sincerity and conviction. He laid no claims to any particular psychic gift. He expressed a desire for as little publicity as possible, and declined any of the great emoluments that could easily have come to him as the result of the enormous interest felt by the public all over the world in these scripts.

---

[1] Lord Northcliffe owned the newspaper 'The Weekly Despatch', and over the period 1920 to 1921 serialised these communications. This created enormous public interest, the vast majority of it was very favourable, and Rev. George Vale Owen was even asked to go down to London to deliver a sermon on them. There did not appear to be any significant theological objections from the Church of England, and in fact it was accepted that these communications were genuine "inspirational writings", that the Rev. G. Vale Owen was genuine, and that the writings were of great value. In spite of this they have all but disappeared from sight today. G.J.C.

Preface (1925)

THIS volume contains the second of a series of communications from beyond the veil received and written down by the Rev. G. Vale Owen, Vicar of Orford, Lancashire.

The messages in this volume are complete in themselves and all are given by one who calls himself Zabdiel and who in the opening line of the messages describes himself as the guide of Mr. Vale Owen.

Following on the communications which Mr. Vale Owen received from his mother,[2] and which terminated on October 30, 1913, in rather an abrupt manner, Mr. Vale Owen again sat in the vestry of the Parish Church, Oxford, on the evening of November 3 and received by automatic writing the words "Zabdiel your guide is here." From that date and until the evening of January 3, 1914, a series of communications amounting to some 60,000 words and occupying some thirty-seven sittings were given by this communicator.

These messages cover a wider range than those the Vicar received from his mother. The inter-relation of this and the afterlife is more fully explained both in narrative and exposition; and in the last message of all the highest note of spiritual rapture is reached.

To criticise or attempt to elucidate these messages from Zabdiel is not my intention in this preface. The mass of information they contain, the new light they throw on the life beyond the veil, and the knowledge that is unfolded respecting spiritual causes which affect our life here must be left to the understanding of each individual who reads this volume.

That these communications come from a source outside the personality of Mr. Vale Owen will be very apparent to those who follow them closely. On the question of the origin of these scripts I am reminded of a letter which Mr. Vale Owen wrote to me regarding a portion of the messages published in The Weekly Dispatch in the latter part of February, 1920, "When I had read the last half-column I put it down with tears in my eyes. I tried it again

---

[2] Published in Volume 1 of The Life Beyond the Veil—The Lowlands of Heaven.

later—same result. It comes from somebody who knows how to get into my soft places. It all bears out what I said to you: 'You are interpreting to me the script for the first time.'"

The Personality of Mr. Vale Owen.

In the London Evening News of July 16, 1920, in the course of a review of the first volume of The Life Beyond the Veil, Sir William Barrett, F.R.S., referring to Mr. Vale Owen, wrote:

"Here we have a beloved and honoured clergyman, whose saintly and devoted life is known to all his parishioners, retiring to the vestry of his church and in the solemn silence of the place finds his hand guided by some unseen power, whilst evening after evening there swiftly written down the record of a pilgrim's progress in the spiritual world. And this record is entirely independent of any conscious or voluntary guidance on his part. Only on two occasions had the Rev. Vale Owen any idea of what subject was to be treated, and often when he had anticipated one topic the writing disclosed a wholly different train of thought.

"Reluctant at first to yield to this involuntary guidance, doubtful of its legitimacy and sceptical of the result, he was at last convinced that the messages were wise and helpful; that they did not originate from his own mind; but appeared to be impressed upon him by some extraneous spirit.

Believing that these messages would afford hope and consolation to many stricken hearts, the author consented to their publication, but, as Lord Northcliffe tells us, he refused to touch a penny of the large emolument he might have had. I wonder how many of the Rev. Vale Owen's critics and detractors—with a family to support, as I am informed is the case here—would have acted in this noble and utterly unselfish way!"

Lord Northcliffe has also drawn particular attention to the question of the personality of Mr. Vale Owen. But although the fierce ray of publicity has penetrated the quietude of the peaceful Vicarage at Orford, Mr. Vale Owen is the last man on earth to whom this would make the slightest material difference. He has always been most emphatic, both in his letters and to all those with whom he has been brought in contact, in stating that it is the messages that are of paramount importance and not the man. It is, however, impossible altogether to accede to the wishes of Mr.

Life Beyond the Veil

Vale Owen in this respect. On Tuesday, June 15, 1920 the Vicar of Orford after considerable pressure was prevailed upon by the Hon. and Rev. James Adderley to preach at St. Paul's Church, Covent Garden, London. The scenes that took place in that famous old London church were described in the Daily Mail the next morning as follows:

"There were all sorts and conditions of people—clergymen, Army officers, City men, girl typists, Covent Garden porters, women in working garb, women of leisure, widows in their weeds, labourers in corduroys. These and other types of humanity were all there. When he left the church Mr. Vale Owen was surrounded by men and women who grasped him by both hands. Men bared their heads and a number of women wept. When Mr. Vale Owen freed himself he stood on the steps and to the hushed assemblage addressed a few simple words. As he descended the steps hundreds of people again rushed to greet him. It was with the greatest difficulty that his friends, clerical and lay, were able to escort him to the rectory across the road. Thousands of people have written to Mr. Vale Owen congratulating him on his writings. Many people in yesterday's congregation travelled specially from the north of England, Manchester and Leeds in particular, to hear his address."

The advent of Mr. Vale Owen to London on this occasion illustrated at once and in a remarkable manner the value of his personality. The Rev. James Adderley, standing beside the altar of St. Paul's, Covent Garden, before pronouncing the benediction, addressed the vast congregation saying:

"With regard to our preacher to-day, we are perfectly certain there is no fraud and no self-advertisement and no denial of Christianity. That is putting it only in a very negative way. I am not saying anything of the positive things we could say. If we had any doubt about it before we have none now, for if ever a man had an opportunity for self-advertisement and fraud our preacher has had it to-day standing in this church, packed from end to end, hundreds of people outside unable to get in; if he had been out for self-advertisement, was it psychologically possible that he could have preached such a sermon as he has to-day? Anybody knows he could not, and knowing that I asked Mr. Vale Owen to preach here because I thought it would do real good to people of all kinds, convinced believers and those who are sceptical, to have an opportunity of seeing a simple-minded humble Christian parson, who does believe in these experiments, and who has had the most extraordinary psychical experiences, of seeing what manner of man he is and of hearing what he has to say. If it has done nothing more, it may make people think a little more, make them wonder whether there is not a new spiritual movement going on in the world and whether any religious person can afford to stand altogether outside or is not bound to come inside it, at least to learn something about it, to discuss it, to inquire into it; because if there is any meaning at all in religion, it means that these things are so real that those who believe in God and Jesus Christ cannot possibly neglect them."

Mr. Vale Owen's World-Wide Correspondence.

As a natural consequence of the world-wide publicity and interest in these scripts during their publication in The Weekly Dispatch and other journals overseas, Mr. Vale Owen has received an enormous number of letters from every part of the globe. Of the great majority expressing gratitude, or making urgent enquiries, many were such as deeply to move him, and also to humble him by bringing realisation of the immense volume of goodwill created. I cannot refrain quoting from a letter written to me by Mr. Vale Owen referring to a certain section of his correspondence, in view of the light it throws on a particular phase of his character. It was in answer to one in which I could not help speaking with indignation on the attitude of certain persons towards the scripts and even towards Mr. Vale Owen himself. Gently rebuking me, he wrote:

"Let us treat our anonymous post-carders and other revilers gently and with patience. They are following, not in a very high-minded way truly, the course they believe to be right and many would be prepared to make sacrifices for their cause—although some are not prepared to do this to the extent of backing up their opinions and convictions by coming out into the open with their names. But viewing the whole matter generally, I cannot but realize what a joy it will be some day, somewhere, to take them by the hand as brothers and sisters and to tell them that we were not too bitter against them when their rather cruel words of misjudgement and attribution of false motives came from them, because we realized that they were but treading the road by which we ourselves had come. That is so in my own case, at least. I see my own former self reflected in their present attitude, and I hope it helps to keep me in humility and in love to them. Indeed, I owe them, for this reason, a debt not of resentment, but of gratitude. I refer not to their bitterness, but to their lack of enlightenment."

This letter is typical of the many that I have received from Mr. Vale Owen, and makes it unnecessary for me to insist on what I venture to call the Christ-like nature of G. V. O., as his parishioners, who are also his friends, his comrades and his followers, dearly love to call him. Of his practical energy and foresight in affairs of his parish, his buoyant cheerfulness and untiring labours, I have already spoken in my preface in Vol. 1.

Manly though his attitude is towards this life and its trials and vicissitudes, and fascinating in every degree as is his personality; I must ask every reader of this volume to respect the wishes of Mr. Vale Owen as far as possible and centre his attention upon the communications of Zabdiel and not on the one who was used as an instrument to give them to the world. H. W. ENGHOLM.

London, September, 1920

General Notes how the Messages Came

In the typewritten copies of the original manuscript, Mr. Vale Owen gave a description of how it came about that he acted as amanuensis for his mother and the spirit beings who in turn took her place at the sittings in the vestry of the church at Orford. He said:

"There is an opinion abroad that the clergy are very credulous beings. But our training in the exercise of the critical faculty places us among the most hard-to-convince when any new truth is in question. It took a quarter of a century to convince me—ten years that spirit communication was a fact, and fifteen that the fact was legitimate and good.

"From the moment I had taken this decision, the answer began to appear. First my wife developed the power of automatic writing. Then through her I received requests that I would sit quietly, pencil in hand, and take down any thoughts which seem to come into my mind projected there by some external personality and not consequent on the exercise of my own mentality.

Highlands of Heaven

Reluctance lasted a long time, but at last I felt that friends were at hand who wished very earnestly to speak with me. They did not overrule or compel my will in any way—that would have settled the matter at once, so far as I was concerned—but their wishes were made ever more plain.

"I felt at last that I ought to give them an opportunity, for I was impressed with the feeling that the influence was a good one, so, at last, very doubtfully I decided to sit in my cassock in the vestry after Evensong.

"The first four or five messages wandered aimlessly from one subject to another. But gradually the sentences began to take consecutive form, and at last I got some which were understandable. From that time, development kept pace with practice. When the whole series of messages was finished I reckoned up and found that the speed had been maintained at an average of twenty-four words a minute. On two occasions only had I any idea what subject was to be treated. That was when the message had obviously been left uncompleted. At other times I had fully expected a certain subject to be taken, but on taking up my pencil the stream of thought went off in an altogether different direction.

"G. V. O."

Before commencing to write Mr. Vale Owen would number a quantity of sheets of paper, these he placed before him on the table in the vestry. Then, using shaded candle-light to illuminate the top sheet of paper and with his pencil in his hand he would wait until he felt the influence to write. When once he started the influence was maintained without a stop until the message for the evening was concluded by the communicator. The words of the message came in a perfectly steady flow and were joined together as if the writer were striving to keep pace with the communication which was being impressed upon his mind. A reproduction of an actual page of the script is given in The Lowlands of Heaven, volume 1 of The Life Beyond the Veil.

H. W. E.

About Zabdiel who Communicated.

In the course of these communications Zabdiel has given

Life Beyond the Veil

no indication as to who he may have been during his earth life or of what period of our earth's history he lived here. To Mr. Vale Owen he always addressed himself as his friend and guardian and his spiritual presence is very real to the Vicar of Orford. I am privileged to be able to give for the first time in these notes the full story of an experience that befell a young woman who attended evening service at the parish church of Orford on Palm Sunday, 1917, and it seems to indicate very directly the presence of Zabdiel on this occasion. I myself have questioned at great length this young girl, Mary A., and her story coupled with the appeal expressed by Mr. Vale Owen to Zabdiel, the same evening, points very clearly to the fact that it was Zabdiel who was seen by the girl and thus came to the help of Mr. Vale Owen in response to his prayer. I give the story from notes made by Mr. Vale Owen himself at the time and I use his own words:

"After Evensong on Palm Sunday, 1917, a girl of about eighteen or nineteen years of age came to me in the vestry. Without any preliminaries she asked,

'Mr. Owen, is there such a thing as seeing angels?'

"I replied, 'Certainly; why?'

"'Because I have seen one.'

"'When?'

"'To-night, in church.'

"She then in answer to further questions explained that just as I had entered the pulpit she saw an angel near the 'Shield,' who passed over the heads of the congregation. As he passed, he turned and smiled—a very beautiful and sweet smile it was—and seemed to go towards me in the pulpit and there disappeared. This was the first experience of the kind she had had, and it gave her so great a shock that she had not recovered from it during the remainder of the service. Indeed, as she spoke to me, she was visibly trembling. I told her that, had she not given way to fright, she would probably have seen him standing with me in the pulpit.

"As to her reference to the 'Shield'; there are six shields on either side of the nave, attached to the corbels. Those on the south are illuminated with ecclesiastical insignia; those on the north with the arms of local families. The third from the chancel arch on the south side is just about half way down the nave, the pulpit stands outside the chancel on the north side.

"The occurrence she related interested me on this particular evening for the following reason:

"On account of extra work owing to the war, I had been feeling very unwell for some weeks past. Palm Sunday is a full day in most parishes, and that evening I was feeling very much spent. As the time for the sermon drew near I began to dread the ordeal and wondered what was going to happen. After saying my usual prayer before going into the pulpit, therefore, I made an appeal to my guide, Zabdiel. I told him I needed his help very really as I did not feel at all equal to the preaching of a sermon without notes, and was in acute pain. So I asked him to give me his help in a special degree that night. What the girl had told me assured me that my request had not been in vain, and it showed me who had brought me the help I already was aware I had received. For on entering the pulpit my pain had suddenly ceased and the preaching was no effort at all. Preoccupation might have explained it had the effect not been so marked and instantaneous. Before Mary A. had spoken to me I had decided that the effect was too great for such a cause, and had already thanked Zabdiel for acceding to my request."

Note by H. W. E. When interviewing Mary A. in reference to the above experience I was very much impressed by the girl's obvious honesty. She is a typical Lancashire lass of the industrial classes, earning her living by working in a metal works. She told me that at the sight of the "angel," as she called the appearance, she was so thoroughly frightened that she bent her head down and clutched at her friend who was seated by her side, and did not dare to leave the pew until the service was over. From her manner in telling of her experience, it was obvious to me that she will never forget it.

A Message from Zabdiel.

On Saturday evening, January 31, 1920, Mr. Vale Owen's wife received a message through the planchette, which instrument had been on various occasions operated by her and through which a considerable number of messages had been given from time to time that proved helpful and instructive to Mr. Vale

Owen when he was receiving the different communications now published. This occasion happened to be on the eve of the publication of the first of the series of the scripts in The Weekly Dispatch. The message was spelt out by the pointer of the planchette, running from letter to letter of the alphabet, written on the board over which the instrument was propelled. I give it here exactly as it was received; it reads as follows:

"'Zabdiel. My son, your Script will be a blessing to the world. Zabdiel gives you his blessing. My son, we lately have done right well, giving you what we can, quietly working with you. When I gave those first writings to you we arranged long ahead what should be done when they came to be published.

Long hours of work you gave to me. Do you think I should leave you to fight the great battle alone?'

'Any more from Zabdiel?'

" 'I have no more to say now except, God bless you all. God's blessings rest upon you in your endeavour to give to the world the truth.'

The Reality of Zabdiel.

During the first week of the publication of the Script in The Weekly Dispatch, the thoughts of thousands of people were turned towards Orford. This quite insignificant village had become famous in a day and was destined to be known throughout the world. No one realized more than Mr. Vale Owen during that momentous week that he had turned his back once and for all on the old order of things and that his outlook on life could never be quite the same again. Controversy about the Scripts was already beginning to rage throughout the country, and the mailbags for the Vicarage were the largest that had ever been seen in that peaceful village of Lancashire. In the midst of this new condition of things I received a letter from the Vicar. A document written straight from the soul of a man who realizes the nature of the high task before him; and its tremendous importance to the world. I publish it because I feel it may be helpful to many who will be reading the messages from Zabdiel for the first time.

Extract from letter addressed to H. W. Engholm, February 11, 1920.

"It has taken me some years to think things out. I have done so and made up my mind. I have been down into the Valley of Decision and wrestled it all out. It was rather dark down there at times. But I have now come out of the Valley and I stand to-day upon the hilltop in the fierce light of day. I have given myself at last but wholly to the Great Cause, and any personal feelings count no more at all with me. So never hesitate to tell me what to do and I will do it gladly. When I went into our little church this morning it was quite dark. I knelt in my little corner, but there was so great a surging of spiritual forces all around that I had to get up and walk up and down the church for a time panting. At last I came to a stand in the chancel and this is what I realized. It was quite distinct and real.

"The whole spirit world near the earth was in motion. It was immense, like the ocean beating against the rocks. High above stood Our Lord the Christ. He was stern and immovable, but He looked down our way and with Him there was a great host of fighting men all ready for the battle, and some were already engaged with the enemy. Between Him and me stood Zabdiel. He stood there straight and tall—taller and more majestic than I had ever realized him before.

His hands were straight down by his sides, clenched and determined as he poured down upon me a great stream of strength and determination which he in turn seemed to be drawing down from those above him. All this while the forces rushed and surged about him and me, but he was quite calm and like the Christ immovable. And as I stood there still, but still panting—for the power was really overwhelming—he gradually came down and stood on my right-hand side. But he towered above me as we stood together there comrades both."

To Mr. Vale Owen, I know, the life to come is a living reality. He feels that he is now carrying out his humble duty to those fair angel friends, whose continual presence strengthens and sustains him night and day, and he will continue to do so until he is called to the presence of the Christ whom he daily strives to serve as a faithful and loving servant. H. W. E.

Angelic Love

I

Open your world to me,

Fair angel friends,

Your world of peace and beauty and delight,

Of people robed in radiance and bedight,(adorned)

On brow and breast and shoulder, with the gem

Of Order and Degree of Ministry

In those broad acres of Eternity

Or here below, as is allotted them.

Open your world to me:

Yet not too broad make the Shekinah beam

To fall upon my poor dull vision yet,

Lest I lose heart by contrast; lest I fret

To leave my duty now, before the theme

Of this my present course be here complete

But just enough to keep and guide my feet

Till this life blends into the Life Supreme,

Fair angel friends.

Highlands of Heaven

II

Open your hearts to me,

Fair angel friends;

Open to me your large, untiring love,

And let me see how placidly you move

Amid the wonders of the Universe,

Where wish is act accomplished; where each breast

Heaves glowing and responsive to the quest

Of kindred spirit seeking to converse.

Open your loves to me—

Yet you will know, your clearer eyes will see

How much 'tis well to give and to withhold—

Lest I to claim for earth be over bold

The license of your larger liberty;

But just a gleam vouchsafe, nor seek to hide

How blest are loves where love is purified;

How our love tends

Toward the love to be,

Fair angel friends.

Life Beyond the Veil

Note.—Subsequent to the reception of the portion of the script which is included in this volume, I received the verses printed above. It was intimated to me, at that time that the purpose for which this hymn was transmitted was that it should be regarded as the keynote to this series of messages.

Preface (1946)

This Script—transmitted by automatic or, more correctly, by inspirational writing—falls into four distinct sections, all, however, forming one progressive whole. It was all, quite evidently, planned out in advance by those who had its transmission in hand.[3]

The link between mother and son was, no doubt, considered the most likely avenue through which to open up communication in the first instance. It was my mother, therefore, and a band of friends who transmitted to me the first part.

The experiment proving successful, another teacher was introduced named Astriel, one of higher rank and of more philosophic mind and diction. The messages given by my mother's band and Astriel form the first book of the Script, The Lowlands of Heaven.

Having passed this test I was handed over to Zabdiel, whose messages are on a higher level than the simpler narrative of my mother. These form The Highlands of Heaven.

The next phase was The Ministry of Heaven, given by one who called himself "Leader," and his band. Subsequently he seems to have assumed, more or less, sole control of communication. Then he speaks of himself as "Arnel." Under this name his narrative, which forms the fourth book, The Battalions of Heaven, is the climax of the whole. His messages are of a more intense nature than any of the foregoing, which were evidently preparatory.

It will be obvious that, in order to obtain the true perspective, the books should be read in the sequence given above. Otherwise some of the references in the later volumes to incidents narrated in the earlier may not be quite clear.

As to the personages concerned in the transmission of the messages : my mother passed into the higher life in 1909, aged sixty-three. Astriel was the Headmaster of a school in Warwick in mid-eighteenth century. Of Zabdiel's earth life I know little or nothing certain. Arnel gives some account of himself in the text.

---

[3] I have located a fifth volume and will also publish that as a Kindle eBook and as a print book. GJC

Highlands of Heaven

Kathleen, who acted as amanuensis on the spirit side, lived in Anfield, Liverpool. She was a seamstress and died, at the age of twenty-eight, about three years before my daughter Ruby who is mentioned in the text and who passed over in 1896 at the age of fifteen months.

How The Messages Came

There is an opinion abroad that the clergy are very credulous beings. But our training in the exercise of the critical faculty places us among the most hard-to-convince when any new truth is in question. It took a quarter of a century to convince me—ten years that spirit communication was a fact, and fifteen that the fact was legitimate and good.

From the moment I had taken this decision, the answer began to appear. First my wife developed the power of automatic writing. Then through her I received requests that I would sit quietly, pencil in hand, and take down any thoughts which seemed to come into my mind projected there by some external personality and not consequent on the exercise of my own mentality. Reluctance lasted a long time, but at last I felt that friends were at hand who wished very earnestly to speak with me. They did not overrule or compel my will in any way—that would have settled the matter at once, so far as I was concerned-—but their wishes were made ever more plain.

I felt at last that I ought to give them an opportunity, for I was impressed with the feeling that the influence was a good one, so, at last, very doubtfully, I decided to sit in my cassock in the vestry after Evensong.

The first four or five messages wandered aimlessly from one subject to another But gradually the sentences began to take consecutive form, and at last I got some which were understandable. From that time, development kept pace with practice. The reader will find the result in the pages following.
G. Vale Owen.
Autumn, 1925.

Introduction

By Sir Arthur Conan Doyle

THE long battle is nearly won. The future may be chequered. It may hold many a setback and many a disappointment, but the end is sure.

It has always seemed certain to those who were in touch with truth, that if any inspired document of the new revelation could get really into the hands of the mass of the public, it would be sure by its innate beauty and reasonableness to sweep away every doubt and every prejudice.

Now world-wide publicity is being given to the very one of all others which one would have selected, the purest, the highest, the most complete, the most exalted in its source. Verily the hand of the Lord is here!

The narrative is before you and ready to speak for itself. Do not judge it merely by the opening, lofty as that may be, but mark the ever ascending beauty of the narrative, rising steadily until it reaches a level of sustained grandeur.

Do not carp about minute details, but judge it by the general impression. Do not be unduly humorous because it is new and strange.

Remember that there is no narrative upon Earth, not even the most sacred of all, which could not be turned to ridicule by the extraction of passages from their context and by over-accentuation of what is immaterial. The total effect upon your mind and soul is the only standard by which to judge the sweep and power of this revelation.

Why should God have sealed up the founts of inspiration two thousand years ago? What warrant have we anywhere for so unnatural a belief?

Is it not infinitely more reasonable that a living God should continue to show living force, and that fresh help and knowledge should be poured out from Him to meet the evolution and increased power of comprehension of a more receptive human nature, now purified by suffering.

All these marvels and wonders, these preternatural happenings during the last seventy years, so obvious and notorious that only shut eyes have failed to see them, are trivial in themselves, but are the signals which have called our material minds to attention, and have directed them towards those messages of which this particular script may be said to be the most complete example.

There are many others, varying in detail according to the sphere described or the opacity of the transmitter, for each tinges the light to greater or less extent as it passes through. Only with pure spirit will absolutely pure teaching be received, and yet this story of Heaven must, one would think, be as near to it as mortal conditions allow.

And is it subversive of old beliefs? A thousand times No. It broadens them, it defines them, it beautifies them, it fills in the empty voids which have bewildered us, but save to narrow pedants of the exact word who have lost touch with the spirit, it is infinitely reassuring and illuminating.

How many fleeting phrases of the old Scriptures now take visible shape and meaning?

Do we not begin to understand that "House with many mansions," and realize Paul's "House not made with hands," even as we catch some fleeting glance of that glory which the mind of man has not conceived, neither has his tongue spoken.

It all ceases to be a far-off elusive vision and it becomes real, solid, assured, a bright light ahead as we sail the dark waters of Time, adding a deeper joy to our hours of gladness and wiping away the tear of sorrow by assuring us that if we are only true to God's law and our own higher instincts there are no words to express the happiness which awaits us.

Those who mistake words for things will say that Mr. Vale Owen got all this from his subconscious self. Can they then explain why so many others have had the same experience, if in a less exalted degree?[4]

I have myself epitomized in two small volumes the general account of the other world, drawn from a great number of sources. It was done as independently of Mr. Vale Owen as his account was independent of mine.

---

[4] I have added a list of reading recommendations at the end which include books similar to this series, but also some I would consider more advanced. This is a very small selection of books on this topic. G.J.C.

Neither had possible access to the other. And yet as I read this far grander and more detailed conception I do not find one single point of importance in which I have erred.

How, then, is this agreement possible if the general scheme is not resting upon inspired truth?

The world needs some stronger driving force. It has been running on old inspiration as a train runs when the engine is removed. New impulse is needed. If religion had been a real compelling thing, then it would show itself in the greatest affairs of all—the affairs of nations, and the late war would have been impossible. What church is there which came well out of that supreme test? Is it not manifest that the things of the spirit need to be restated and to be recoupled with the things of life?

A new era is beginning. Those who have worked for it may be excused if they feel some sense of reverent satisfaction as they see the truths for which they laboured and testified gaining wider attention from the world.

It is not an occasion for self-assertion, for every man and woman who has been honoured by being allowed to work in such a cause is well aware that he or she is but in agent in the hands of unseen but very real, wise, and dominating forces. And yet one would not be human if one were not relieved when one sees fresh sources of strength, and realizes the all-precious ship is held more firmly than ever upon her course.

[Signature Shown}

INTO THE LIGHT

The good God is, and God is good,
And when to us 'tis dimly seen
'Tis but the mists that come between
Like darkness round the Holy Rood,
Or Sinai Mount where they adored
The Rising Glory of the Lord.
He giveth life, so life is good,
As all is good that He has given.
Earth is the vestibule of Heaven;
And so He feeds with angel's food
Those in His likeness He has made,
That death may find us unafraid.
Death is no wraith, of visage pale,
Out of this darkened womb of Earth,
But waits attendant on our birth
To lead us gently through the Veil,
To realms of radiance, broad and free,
To Christ and immortality.

September, 1915.

Note. Subsequent to the reception of the portion of the script which is included in this volume, I received at three separate sittings the verses printed above. It was intimated to me, at that time, that the purpose for which this hymn was transmitted was that it should be regarded as a keynote to the messages received some years previously from my mother and her fellow-workers. G. V. O.

Chapter 1

Divine Love—Human blindness.—Evil and good—Evolution—Unity in diversity.

Monday, November 3, 1913.

ZABDIEL, your guide, is here and would speak with you.
I shall be glad if he will be good enough to do so.[5]
I am able now for the first time, friend, to join in these messages which your mother and her friends are giving through you to your fellows. Now the time has come when I may continue to develop, with your help, the instructions given you, if it be your wish so to continue.

I am much indebted to you, sir. Please tell me what is your wish now.
That you sit and write down my messages, here and at this time, as you have done for the past few weeks for your mother and her friends.

Will my mother, then, cease and give place to you?
Yes, that is her wish. From time to time, however, you shall hear of her, and from her and others of your circle of friends.

And what is the nature of your projected course of instruction?
That of the development of evil and good, and of God's present and future purpose with the Church of the Christ and, throughout, of mankind generally.

It is for you, my friend and charge, to say whether you will proceed, or cease here and go no further. I warn you that, although I shall observe the rule here held advisable of leading onward rather than revealing by cataclysm, yet much that I shall have to say will be of a nature disturbing to you for a time until you have assimilated it and have come to understand the logical sequence of the teaching I shall have to impart.[6]

---

[5] All questions put by Mr. Vale Owen are in italics. —H.W.E.

[6] Compared to several other resources suggested in the recommended reading, this series seems to be the least threatening to those who still

Highlands of Heaven

What of those messages I have received from my mother and her friends?[7] Are they to cease? They are incomplete—there is no proper conclusion to them.

Yes, they will stand very well as they have been given to you. Remember, they were not meant to be in the form of a complete history or a novel. Scrappy they may be, but not unhelpful to those who read with a right mind.

I confess I am rather disappointed at the ending, it is so abrupt. Lately something was said about publication. Is it your wish that they should go forth as they are?

That we leave to your own discretion. Personally I do not see why they should not. I may tell you, however, that this writing you have been doing lately, as all former writing you have received from us, is preparatory to a further advance—which I now propose to you.

When do you wish to begin?

Now; and you may proceed as you are able from day to day, as you already have done. I know your work and your engagements and shall order my own accordingly, so far as my work with you is concerned.

Yes, I will do my best. But I confess, quite candidly, I fear the task. What I mean is, I do not feel developed enough, for, from what you say, sir, there is some pretty stiff mental work afoot in what you propose.[8]

My grace shall be sufficient in the strength of our Lord the Christ, as heretofore.

Well, then, will you begin by telling me something more than I know about yourself?

---

hold fast to orthodox Christian teachings. And if that was its aim, it succeeded admirably. —G.J.C

[7] Referring to the messages received from Mr. Vale Owen's mother, which form part of The Lowlands of Heaven, the first volume of the "Life Beyond the Veil" series.— H.W.E.

[8] Ironically the challenge is as much about soul development as it is about controlling the interference of the mind with its firmly held beliefs. Only those with adequate soul development can receive high level spiritual material. And an ability to set aside previously held beliefs is vital if the medium is to be capable of receiving that which he does not currently believe. These concepts are well explained in the Padgett Messages.—G.J.C.

Life Beyond the Veil

It is not on myself that I would fix your mind, friend, but on the messages proceeding through me to you, and through you to our fellow-Christians fighting their way through the mists of controversy and doubt and misdirected zeal. I want to help them and you, my charge; and to such as have shall be given, and these shall hand it on to others. It is for you still to choose.

I have already chosen. I said so. If you are good enough, Zabdiel, to use a poor instrument like me, that is your business, not mine. I will do my best.

I can only promise so much as that.

Now, what of yourself?

My mission is of more importance than my own personality which will best be delineated through the thoughts I am able to give you. The world is suspicious of one who claims more than they can understand. They believe when they read, "I am Gabriel who stand in the Presence," because that was said long ago. But if I should say to you, "I am Zabdiel who comes to you from High Places with a message from those who are accounted in the Heavenly Realms as Holy Ones and Princes of Love and Light"—well, you know, my friend and charge, what shape their lips would take. And so I pray you let me speak, and judge me and us by what message I am charged with—whether it be true and high or no—and it will suffice for you and for me. One day, dear friend, you shall look on me as I am, and know me better in that day, and be glad.

Very well, sir, I leave it to you. You know my limitations. I am neither clairvoyant nor clairaudient nor a psychic in any real way, I take it. But what has already been written, I admit, has convinced me that it is external to myself,—I think I am convinced that far. So, if you will, I will. I cannot say more, and I know I am not offering you much.

It is enough, and what you lack I must endeavour to supply of my own strength. Now, I will say no more at this time, for I know you have to go; you have work to do. God be with you, my charge, in the Lord Christ Amen.†[9]

Tuesday, November 4, 1913.

---

[9] Zabdiel always concluded his communications with the sign of the Cross.—H.W.E.

May grace and peace be yours, friend, and quietness of mind.

In order that what I have to say be not misunderstood, I would begin by telling you that in these realms we do not dwell so much on those things which are not of immediate importance but search out such matters as most concern our present onward way, master them, and so proceed from step to step on firm and sure ground. Truly, the things of infinity are not altogether absent from our minds—the nature and presence of the Absolute and Ultimate One, and those conditions which are about Him, these are not altogether thrust aside. Yet we are content to let them rest not understood, knowing, as we judge from our own experience in these lower realms, that those beyond us must hold for us blessing even greater than our present state. And so we go onward in perfect trust and confidence, happy to advance, and yet not impatient of the future towards which we surely move. So when I tell you of evil and good I shall deal more of those things which we are able to make plain to you, and these will be but as one dewdrop is to a rainbow, and less than this indeed.

There are those who say there is no evil. These are in error. If evil is the negative of positive good, it is real as the good is real. For it were as rational to say there were no such condition as night, but that this is but the negative aspect of light and day, as to say that evil is not and yet good is. For both are conditions of attitude which individual beings assume toward the One Who Is, and, as each attitude is a qualifying medium of an appropriate effect, so a condition of rebellion is the secondary cause of trouble and disaster to the rebel.

Divine Love.[10]

The very intensity of the Love of God becomes awe-inspiring when it meets with an opposing obstacle. The swifter the torrent the greater the surf about the opposing rocks.

---

[10] Note:—The sub-headings used from this page onwards are, of course, not in the original script, but are simply employed to break up the material into clauses for easier reference.—H.W.E.

The greater the heat of a fire the more complete the dissolution of the fuel which is cast into it, and on which it feeds. And although to some such words may seem horrible in the saying of them, yet it is the very intensity of the Love which energizes and flows through the creation of the Father which, meeting opposing and, disharmonious obstruction, causes the greater pain.

Even in the earth life you may test and prove this true. For the most bitter of all remorse and repentance is that which follows on the realization of the love borne to us by the one we have wronged.

This is the fire of hell, and none else. And if this do not make hell a reality, then what thing could? We who have seen know that only on repentance and the realization that all God's actions are acts of love do the pangs of hell descend upon the sinner, and not until then in their full intensity.

Human Blindness.

But if this be so, if evil be real, then also are evil beings real. Blindness is inability to see. But not only is there such a condition as blindness; there are also people who are blind. Blindness is also a negative condition, or less. It is the condition of one who has four senses instead of five.

But real it is, nevertheless. Yet it is only when one who is born blind is told of the sense of sight that be begins to feel his lack of it, and the more he understands the lack of it the more his lack is felt. So it is with sin. It is usual here to call those who are in the darkness the "undeveloped." This is not a negative term, which would be "retrogressed." So of both I say not "loss" but "lack." The one born blind has not lost a faculty but lacks it.

The sinner also rather lacks than loses his faculty to apprehend the good. His is rather the condition of the blind from birth than the blind from misadventure.

And herein is the explanation of the words of St. John that they who have been brought into the knowledge of the truth cannot sin—not as theoretically considered, but as practically considered. For it is difficult to see how they who have enjoyed the light and all the beauty it reveals should put out their eyes and so become blind.

Those, therefore, who sin do so from lack of knowledge, and inability to appreciate the good and beautiful, and as the blind come to disaster unless they be warded by those who can see—guides either incarnate or discarnate—so with those who are spiritually blind.

Yet you may say that people do go back and fall from grace. Those who do so are such as those who are partly blind or of imperfect sight—colour-blind as to one or more colours. These have never seen perfectly, and their lack is only unknown to them until opportunity offers, and then their imperfection is manifest. For a colour-blind person is one whose sight is, in little or more measure, undeveloped. It is only by using his vision that he maintains what vision he has, and if he neglects to do this then he retrogresses. So with the sinner.

But it may perplex you to be told that many who live apparently good and upright lives on earth are found here among the undeveloped. Yet so it is. They have gone through life with many of their higher spiritual faculties undeveloped, and when they step into the world where all is spiritual, their lack is seen, and only gradually do they come to understand what they have lacked unknowing so long,—just as many colour-blind people live their lives and pass hence and never know their imperfect state of vision; which also is hidden from their fellows.

Suppose you give me a case by way of illustration?

One who teaches the truth in part only must learn here to teach it whole. Quite a large number of people accept the fact of inspiration, but deny that it is an ordinary and perpetual means of God's grace for men. When they come over here they, in turn, become inspirers, if so qualified, and then learn by how much they were indebted in their earthly course to those who used this method with them unknown. They must first develop this lacking knowledge and then they may progress, and not till then.

Now, evil is the antithesis of good, but both may be present, as you know, in one person. It is only by freewill that that person is held responsible for both good and evil in his heart. Of this freewill, and the nature and use of it, I must further speak at another time.

God be with you, friend, and keep you in His Grace. Amen.

†

Life Beyond the Veil

Saturday, November 8, 1913.

Evil and Good.

If you will give me your mind now for a little while I will endeavour to continue my words in reference to the problem of evil and its relation to that which is good. These are indeed relative terms and neither of them absolute as considered from the point of view of a man on earth. For it is not possible that one in whom both have a part be able to define either perfectly, but only, or chiefly, as the effect of each is seen in its working.

Also let it be remembered that what seems to be good or evil to one man does not of necessity so appear in the eyes of another. Especially is this true of those of different creed and habit of thought and manner of life in community. What, therefore, is possible in the matter of distinction between these two is that the broad and fundamental principles which underlie each should be grasped clearly, and the minor shades of these qualities be entrusted to the future when they will be gradually made more plain.

Now, evil is rebellion against those laws of God which are manifest in His working. It is the endeavour of a wise man that he should walk in the same direction as that towards which these laws flow. He who from wilfulness or ignorance opposes this current finds at once that an obstacle is presented to him, and if he persists in his opposition, then disaster will ensue.

For the Life of the Supreme, which operates and energizes through creation, is a force which to oppose leads to destruction. And if a man were powerful enough in himself to bring such opposition to stand in the way of that tremendous force as would check, even for a moment, its flow, annihilation would be his lot when the pent-up energy once again burst forth upon him. But no man is able thus, and to this degree, to oppose God; and it is therefore that our weakness itself is our surety against annihilation such as this.

For a longer or shorter period sometimes, and often indeed for some thousands of years, as you reckon time on earth, a man may maintain his obduracy.

But no man is created who is able to continue so everlastingly. And that is a merciful limit which our Father Creator has placed around and in us lest He lose us, or any one of His children, away from Him, and without return for ever.

Let us therefore, having looked on this phase of aberration from man's natural walking with God, now look the other way in the direction in which all things are tending. For truly, evil is but a transitory phase and, whether it pass away from His economy in whole or no, from every individual most surely it will pass away when its opposing force is spent, and he be left free to follow on in the glorious train of those who brighten as they go from glory to further and greater glory.

For this reason also will the Kingdom of the Christ one day be altogether purged of evil, because individuals make up that Church and, when the last has been ingathered, then will it be complete in its radiating glory to minister perhaps, and as many here believe, to other worlds in need of such help and succour as your world is to-day.

Evolution.

As we stand on the earth plane, where I stand now, and look through the veil of difference of condition which is between us and you in the earth life, we often see many people at one time, and sometimes but few. These people differ in brightness according to the degree of holiness in each; that is, according to the degree in which each individual in himself is able to reflect the divine light of spirit which streams past and through us to you. Some appear very dim, and these, when they come over here, will go to regions dim or less dim according to their own dimness.

As a result everyone will both appear to others and others will appear to him, as natural to the particular environment and atmosphere in which their lot is cast. This is "their own place." Let me illustrate this in order to make it more plain to you. If an electric spark be projected into thick darkness the contrast is too great to appear congruous. We should say that that spark was out of its proper element, and created a disturbance amid the darkness which brought, just for a minute, things to a standstill. Men groping their way along the dark country lane stand still and rub their eyes until they can see to pursue their way once more.

The night animals also for a moment are startled and cease to move.

But if that flash be projected into the atmosphere in the daylight of noon, the disturbance is less, and if it could be projected into the sun it would there lose contrast and blend with his brightness.

So those whose radiance is great go into those spheres whose brightness agrees with their own; and every one into the sphere which agrees with his—be it less or more. But those whose bodies—spiritual bodies I mean—are of gross texture, and do not radiate much light, but are dim, go into those dim spheres where only they may be so much at ease that they may work out their own salvation. They are not at ease indeed in any sense of the word; but only they would be less at ease in a brighter sphere than in those dim regions until they have grown in brightness themselves.

All who pass over here from the earth have some of the darkness which envelops it like a thick pall of mist. But many of these have already in their wills endeavoured to rise through that mist into the clearer realms: and these do quickly here what they would have had difficulty doing below.

And now we are looking upward, and there indeed lies the Royal Road, the King's Highway to His Holy City and the Dwelling Place of His present Majesty.

Along that way we follow step by step; and every step we go we see that far away the light increases ever, and our comrades and ourselves grow in brightness, as in beauty, the further we go. And it is a matter of no small joy that we are permitted, for periods differing according to the needs of you on earth, to come back on our steps and help you on the road we know to be so radiant and so full of the Beauty of His Presence.

And this, my friend and ward, we will endeavour, if you still keep of the mind you are at this present time. I think you will so persevere. But know you that many do set out and then, distrusting the brightness because it dazzles their unaccustomed eyes, turn back to paths more dim where their sight is less challenged. And so we look upon them as they go, and sigh, and turn to seek another, if perchance he should prove strong to bear more of our brightness than the one for whose return here in our ways we must await, till the due time shall come to us and him.

God keep your feet that they do not slip, and your eyes that they be not dimmed, and, although in words of earth you will not be able to write down what you may know, yet so much of it will we endeavour that you write that others may be led so to ask that they may have, so to seek that they shall find, and (if they be very courageous—these two cities being taken) so to dare as to knock, and so to knock that that Gate be opened and the brightness and glory within revealed. †

Monday, November 10, 1913.

As I stand on the plane of earth, above and beyond lie the spheres, into some of which I have penetrated, and of the Tenth of which I am a member. These spheres are not so much what would correspond to localities on earth, but rather estates of life and power, according to the development of the individual. You have already received some instruction as to the multiplicity of these spheres of power, and I do not propose to pursue my own along those lines. I would rather lift your mind into the realms of light and activity by another channel, and this I now proceed to do.

All that is good is potent to accomplish things in two directions. By the power within, a good man, be he incarnate or discarnate, can and does both lift up that which is below him, and also draw down that which is above; not alone as by prayer, but also, of his own right, by power.

Now, this is by reason of his attunement to the Divine Will; for by so much as he is able to correspond with his Divine environment, by so much is he able to work through that environment; that is, to energize and to accomplish things. The things he may so accomplish are manifold even to one who has risen only into a small number of spheres, and these things, when projected through the Veil into your earth life, are accounted wonderful.

For instance. There are here such as have charge of the elements which condition the earth and those things which grow upon the earth. Let us take one example which will serve to illustrate the others: Those who have charge of vegetation.

These are under one Mighty Prince; and are divided and subdivided into departments, all in perfect order. Under these again are others of lower estate who carry out their work under direction, and in conformity to certain unalterable laws laid down in the higher spheres. These are what you know as elemental spirits, and are multiple in number and in form.

The laws of which I speak are very complex the further we proceed from the sphere of their origin; but if we could trace them up-stream and arrive at their origin we should find, I think, that they were few and simple, and at last, in the source and spring of their origin, unity. Of this I, who have been only a little way, can but reason on what I have observed in my upward progress; and this would lead me to hazard that the one law, or principle, from which all the lesser laws and principles are radiated might best be described by the word Love. For, understood as we understand things, Love and

Unity are not much diverse, if not actually identical. We have discovered this much at least, that everything which divides in all the regions and estates on this our own level, and in those spheres below us down to the earth sphere, is in one way or another an abnegation of Love in its most intense and truest meaning.

Unity in Diversity.

But this is a most difficult problem to discuss with you here and now; for it would be very difficult to explain to you how all the diversity you see around you is due, as it seems to us, to this same disintegrating action, and yet is all so wonderfully wise and so beautiful. Still, if you substitute for the word negation the idea of Unity less one part, and then Unity less two parts, and so on, you may perchance get some glimmer of what philosophy is held among us on this subject of Unity radiating into diversity of operativeness.

Although the activity of these lower orders is all regulated by law, yet a great amount of freedom is found within its bounds. And this is to us a matter of much charm because, as you will agree, there is much beauty in diversity, and in the ingenuity displayed by those who energize among plant life.

Some of these laws which govern the elementals and those above them I am unable to understand yet. Some I do understand but am unable to transmit to you. But a few I may tell you, and you will, in your own proper time, learn more as you progress in these heavenly mansions.

It would seem, then, that one rule they must observe in their work is that, having planned out any scheme of development for a family of plants, that scheme must be pursued, in its main elements and essentials, to its natural consummation. All their armies of subordinates are kept within the limits of that unalterable law of evolution. If an oak family is planned, then an oak family that must remain. It may evolve into subdivisions, but these must be subdivisions of the oak. It must not be allowed to branch off into the fern family, or seaweed. These also will be developed along their own line.

Another law is that no department of spiritual workers shall be able to negate the operations of another. They may not, and often do not, work in conformity; but their operations must be along lines of modification, rather than absolute negation, which would mean destruction.

Thus we find that if the seed of two plants of the same family be mixed the result will be a mule plant, or a blend, or a modification. But the seed of one family being mixed with that of another family is without effect. And in neither case is the effect annihilation.

A parasite may entwine itself around a tree. But then ensues a fight. In the end the tree is usually worsted and pays the penalty of defeat. But it is not suddenly laid low. The fight proceeds, and indeed sometimes the tree wins. But it is recognized here that those who invented and carried out the parasitic idea have in the main won the battle of forces.

Thus the war goes on, and when you view it from this side you will see how very interesting it all is.

And now I must tell you something which I have hinted already, and which you may find difficult of acceptance. All these main principles, even when diverse in action, are planned in spheres higher than my own by high and powerful Princes who hold their commission secure under others higher still, who hold theirs from others above them.

I use the word "diverse" in preference to "antagonistic," for among those High Ones antagonism does not find a place, but diversity of quality in wisdom does, and is the cause of the wonderful diversity in nature as it works out in its procession from those Higher Heavens outward through the lower spheres into that of matter which is visible to you on earth. Where antagonism enters is in those spheres where the radiating wisdom has become more attenuated by reason of its journey outward in every direction through spheres of innumerable myriads of freewilled beings, and diluted and refracted in its passage.

And yet, when you consider the stars of different size and complement, and the waters of the sea, naturally still but by the motion of the earth and the gravitation of bodies at a distance is allowed to have no rest; and then the more rarefied atmosphere which, also responding to the pulls and pushes of the forces which impinge upon the earth, whips into motion the heavier liquid; and all the diversity of form and colour of grass and plant and tree and flower and insect life and life more evolved, the birds and animals, and of the continuous movement among them all; and the way in which they are permitted one to prey upon another, and yet not to annihilate wholly, but every species must run its race before it pass away—all this and more; then will you not, my ward and friend, confess that God is indeed most wonderful in the manner of His working, and that the wonder justifies most fully the measures He has permitted His higher servants to adopt and use, and the manner also of their using?

In His Holy Name I bless you, friend—and that is peace. †

Chapter 2

Men and Angels

Degrees of light in the spheres—Geometrical astronomy—The orbit of human life—Angel visitants to earth—The wrestling of Jacob—The power of a name—Courage in thinking—The Divinity of the Christ—Love and its opposite—"Now we see through a glass darkly"—Zabdiel's Heavenly Home.

Wednesday, November 12, 1913.

IF it were possible, friend that we should be so united as to be enabled to look out on things from one point of view and vantage, these matters in hand would be so much the easier to explain. But you look hence from one side the Veil which hangs between things and the region of their causation, and I from the other side. So that our outlook is normally in opposition, and when I would make things appear simple to you I must perforce turn me about and look the other way and, so far as I am able, with your eyes rather than my own.

This doing so far as in me lies, therefore, I call you to gaze with me into the upward reaches of creation, inversely to their natural course and flow from the High Ones outward towards the spheres where what is material begins to assume and claim a place.

As we go we find that what things we have known as belonging to our environment in the lower spheres begin to assume other aspects: they are transformed to the vision, and transubstantiated to the sense of inward perception, and yet are related to those things which obtain in the sphere of matter, or those next above as the sun is related to the twilight of earth.

Degrees of Light in the Spheres.

Taking first this same matter of light. Light is known on earth by reason of its contrast with darkness, which is merely a state of absence of light, and intrinsically of no content or value. So that when we speak of darkness we mean a lack of certain

Highlands of Heaven

vibrations which enable the retina of the eye to register the presence of external things.

Now in the regions of spiritual darkness on this side of the Veil a like condition of affairs also obtains. For those who are in darkness are those whose sense of sight lacks the vibrations from without which enable others to have knowledge of those things which to them are external but present withal. Their state is a state of inability to receive these vibrations. When their spiritual faculties do undergo change then they are able to see more or less clearly.

But also these vibrations which convey the knowledge of things to their sense of sight are, in those regions, of a more gross quality than in the regions of spiritual health. So that even to those good spirits who penetrate into those regions, and whose sense of sight is more perfect, yet the darkness is quite apparent, and the light by which they see is dim. So that, as you will understand, there is response between the spirit and the spirit's environment, and that response is so accurate and perpetual and sustained as to constitute a permanent state of life.

As we go higher in the spheres this responsive action between the spirits and their environment is also maintained and that which we may call the external light becomes more and more perfect and intense the higher we go. So it is that those who dwell in, as we will say, the Fourth Sphere may not penetrate into the Fifth, to remain there, until they have become so developed as to sustain with ease the degree of intensity of light there obtaining. Having attained to that Fifth Sphere they soon become used to its light. And if they return to the Fourth, as they do from time to time, that Fourth Sphere seems dimmer to them, while still they are able to see with comparative ease. But if they should descend straight to the Second or First Sphere, they would only with difficulty be able to use those denser vibrations of light and, in order to do so, are obliged to train themselves to see in that same sphere which once was but their normal abode.

When we come down to your earth sphere we see by reason of the spiritual light which men have in themselves. And those who are of higher spiritual grade than others we see so much the more clearly.[11]

---

[11] This is a curious matter, and one which for a long time I suspected was

Were it not for faculties we possess other than that of sight, we should, as I suppose, have difficulty in finding our way about, and to those to whom we wish to come. But we have these other faculties, and by their use are able to do our work in ministering to you.

You will now be able to understand that there is a quite literal truth in the words, "Who dwells in light which no man can approach." For few in the earth life are able to rise many spheres beyond; and the light which streams from above is blinding even to those who are much progressed.

Now think what of beauty this evermore perfect light implies. You have colours on earth which to mortal eyes are entrancing. Just over the border on this side are colours which are much more beautiful and more varied. What then must be the beauty in this one thing alone as we advance into the greater light! Even what I myself have seen, who have only come this little way, is more than I can even hint at in this language in which I am trying to speak to you now, and which to-day is as a foreign tongue to me, who am also limited to the use of what store of words you yourself possess.[12]

But those who love beauty will find a never-failing supply to their great joy and, as light and holiness go hand in hand, so, as they progress in the one, will they in the larger enjoyment of the other. This is the Beauty of Holiness, and it is past all imagination of mortal men. But it is worthy of meditation, and if you will keep it in mind then what things are beautiful on earth will speak to you more really of the greater beauties of the Heavenly Realms where the joy of life is all one can desire. Which one day shall be yours, good friend, if you keep in the right and onward way. †

---

true of all levels in the spirit world. The first time I came across the topic was in the book *Letters from the Light* and it is an example of a not very advanced spirit making a statement that is only true of the low level he inhabits. He claimed it to be a self-lighted realm, whereas that appears to only be true of the darker spheres. G.J.C.

[12] This is an aspect of mediumship that few people seem to know. Spirit can access memories we can no longer access ourselves, even repeating word for word something we have read. But it also means that to receive high level scientific material, a medium trained in that specific subject is essential. G.J.C.

Highlands of Heaven

Geometrical Astronomy.

Saturday, November 15, 1913

And now, my friend and ward, I would that I might enable you to see one other matter from this standpoint where I stand, and that is the real relation of spirit power and energy to the phenomena of development among the heavenly bodies as men of science have observed them and tabulated them and, reckoning up their joint message, have made their deductions, and from these have, with some penetration and wisdom, formulated the laws according to which these things come about.

The term "heavenly bodies" has a dual significance and will be interpreted according to the measure and quality of the individual mind. To some these orbs are creatures of the heavens material, and to others they are none else but manifestations and results of the energizing of spirit life. The mode of operation of this spirit life, also, is not understood by all alike; and by some the term is used most vaguely. To say that God made all things is to say a big thing in few words. But the significance of the truth herein embodied is somewhat tremendous; and for all but those who are able to rise into clearer light than that which hovers about the dim places of the earth plane, it would be nearer the truth to say that herein is a truth not so much embodied as entombed. Out of the simplest wisdom are made the greatest things; and out of the most elementary of geometrical figures arise the most wonderful combinations of perpetual movement. For it is only the purest and simplest things that are competent to be used most freely and without entanglement. And this state of affairs alone gives warrant of perpetuity, whether on earth, or in the vast reaches of space through which go these worlds and systems, eternally because perfectly ordered in their course.

Now, it is not too much to say that the appointed paths of all these bodies of the heavenly systems are shaped of two principles: that of the right line, and that of the curve. It is even more true and exact to say that their orbits may be said to be shaped out of one form only, and that the right line itself. All go onward impelled in a right and straight course and yet not one that is known to us but travels in a curve. Astronomers will explain why this is, but I will note one instance by way of example here.

The earth, we will suppose, is set forth on its journey. It travels in a straight line from one point. That is its potential movement. But directly it leaves that point it begins to fall towards the sun, and we find after a while that it is moving in an ellipse. There is no straight line here, but a series of curves worked together in one figure, which is the orbit of the earth.

And yet the pull of the sun was not in the fashion of a curve, but in a right line, direct. It was the combination of these two straight lines of energy—the impetus of the earth and the gravitation of the sun—which, being perpetually exerted, bent the orbit of the earth from a straight into an elliptical shape, and one in which many elements of curve entered to build it up complete. I leave out other influences which modify this once again in order to concentrate your mind on this one great principle. I put it in formula thus: Two straight lines of energy operating on one another produce a closed curve.

Both, you will note, are quite orderly in their working; and both are beautiful and of wonderful power. For, that any body of matter move at all should seem Wonderful, and is so in truth. Yet each modifying the other, and the greater dominating the lesser without depriving it of its essential power and freedom of movement, these by their joint action—exerted and directed apparently in opposition—produce a figure of greater beauty than the two straight lines, which are as the parents to the child.

Now, you would not, I take it, say because these forces are seen to be exerted against one another that this is a bad scheme and plan whose origin is of evil. For you see these two bodies still continuing their journey through space year after year, and century after century, and you come to think it rather a matter for awe and reverence than for contempt. It displays a Wisdom which is beautiful in its working and mighty in operation; and you praise God Whose mind conceived all this, for He must be very wise and very great indeed. And you do well.

The Orbit of Human Life.

Yet when His other works you contemplate, but understand them not so well as this, sometimes you men are too ready to doubt Him and His ways of working. You see a like opposition of forces in human life, and you say His plan is here imperfect. You think He might have made a better way; and many doubt His wisdom and His love because, seeing but a minute section of the curve of the great orbit of existence, they cannot but conclude that all is falling, falling to destruction; or at least that a straight and right line would be the better course, and not these combinations which curve the impetus of human life from its direct onward way of evolution: without disaster and without pain.

My dear friend and ward, these things might be otherwise than as they are, but they would not be near so lovely in their completed orbit then as they will be in the path on which He Who made all and sees the end of things sent them forth. These forces which in opposition produce straining and travail and pain are as those which make the orbit of the earth what it is; and He Who sees the perfect form has seen it well to work thus, and in patience looks on towards the consummation of this His perfect scheme.

We here do see not all nor much of the road ahead; yet more than you we see, and so much as enables us to content ourselves and press onward, helping others on the road, content and trusting that all will be well ahead however far we go. For now we do not seek with much labour to reckon on the course we are travelling wrapped round with earth mist which hinders us to see, but we view the way from the clear sunlight atmosphere of these heavenly realms; and I tell you the orbit of human life, as it works out towards completion, is beautiful too, so beautiful and so lovely that we are often brought to arrest in wondering awe at His Majesty of Love and blended Wisdom, to Whom we bow in lowly adoration not to be expressed in any words of mine, but only in the, yearning of my heart. Amen, and my blessing upon you, friend. Look up and be fearless for, believe me, all is fair ahead and all is well. †

Monday, November 17, 1913.

"What thou seest write in a book." These words were spoken by an Angel to John in Patmos, and he carried out the command as he was able. He wrote his account and handed it to his brethren; and from a time till now men have striven to wrest from that account its meaning. They have tried one method and another, and confess themselves perplexed. Yet their perplexity is of their own making, friend, for had they read as little children read they would have been able to turn the door with the right key, and to enter into the Kingdom to see what beauties there await such as are able to take a simple man's simple words simply, and believe.

But men have loved perplexity ever, and seek in it to find profundity and depth of wisdom. And they fail, for, looking on the surface of the glass, they are dazzled and blinded at the reflected light, which they should have looked through and beyond at the glories there revealed.

So do men add perplexity to perplexity and call it knowledge. But knowledge is in no wise perplexing, but the lack of it is. So when I seek to explain anything to you, and through you to others, do you not look so much on the surface of things, at the precise method by which this comes to pass; and do not start in doubt at words and phrases familiar to you as your own, for these are my material by which I build up my house; and only such as I find stored in your mind can I use.

Moreover, all these years past you have been watched and prepared, partly to this very end, that we should use you thus, and that where we lack, for further contact with your material sphere, there you yourself should come to our aid. We can show you things—you must write them down. Thus what thou seest write in a book, and send it forth to be dealt with by men, each according to the measure of his own capacity, and each as his faculties are quickened to the perception of spiritual things. Let that suffice, then. Come with us and we will tell you what we are able.

You say "we." Are there others besides?

Angel Visitants to Earth.

We work all together, friend. Some are here present with me bodily, others still in their several spheres are able to send forth their help from those realms without their leaving them. Also there is a certain help which only may be given thus. For you will know that, as the diver at the bottom of the sea must be tended with air by those above continually for his support, so it is likewise helpful that we be ministered to while we also minister. By this we are enabled the more clearly to speak to your mind of the higher verities while we stand on this dim and grosser lower plane as on the bed of the ocean where our natural air is scanty and our light looms far above. Think of it and us in this way and you will be able to understand a part of our task.

Some there are who ask why angels do not come in plenty nowadays as in the olden times. Here are many errors in few words, and two pre-eminent. For first, angels of high estate did never come in plenty to the earth plane, but one here and another there amid the ages; and those were accounted worthy of a forward place in the annals of great events. Angels do not in this way come to earth and visibly appear, except it be on some very rare and special commission. This was an extension of our difficult task: first the diver must get to the dark and very deep waters, and then he must so condition himself that he is visible to those nearly blind creatures whose habitat is on the ocean floor.

No; we work for men, and are present with them, but in other ways than this, according to rule and varying method as each task requires. And that is the second error made; for we are present and do come to earth continually. But in that word "come" more lies hidden than I may reveal. For even those on this side, in the spheres between us and you, do not understand yet our powers and the ways of their using, but only in part as they learn in the course of their progress. And so let it rest thus. And now I will explain to you another matter of interest.

The Wrestling of Jacob.

The audience which Jacob had of the Angel at Jabbok when he wrestled with him and prevailed: What, think you, was that wrestling; and what was the reason of the withholding of the Angel's name?

I think that the wrestling was a bodily wrestling; and that Jacob was allowed to prevail in order to show him that his wrestling with his own nature during his residence in Padan Aram had not been in vain—that he had prevailed. I think the Angel withheld his name because it was not lawful to give it to a man still in the flesh.

Well, the first answer is better than the second, which, my charge, is not saying a very great deal. For, see you, if he did not give it because it was not lawful to give, why was it not lawful?

Now, the wrestling was real and actual, but not form to

form as men do usually wrestle. The Angel might not be touched by mortal hands with impunity. He had manifested in visible form, and that form was even tangible, but not rudely to be treated. For the power of that Angel was such that the mere touching of the thigh of Jacob produced dislocation. What then would have happened if Jacob had taken that form within his arms? But the Angel was held there by the will of Jacob: not because Jacob's was the stronger will, but because of the Angel's condescension and courtesy. While Jacob wished he stayed, but courteously asked to be permitted to go. Do you wonder at this great indulgence? Think of the Christ of God and His humiliation among men and you will wonder no longer. Courtesy is one of the outward manifestations of love, and may not be disregarded in that long course of training which makes us what we are and do become.

So was the Angel held because he gave that much. But Jacob is not so charming. In him his newly realized strength of will and character overbears his finer sentiments for the time, and demands a blessing. This he obtains, but not the Angel's name.

The Power of a Name.

It were not quite accurate to say it was not lawful that it should be given. Sometimes the names are given. But in this case not; and for this reason: There is much power in the use of a name. Know this, and remember it; for much disaster continually ensues by reason of the misuse of holy names, disaster wondered at and often felt to be unmerited. Jacob for his own sake was denied that name. He had shown his willingness to demand a blessing, but must not be given to be enabled to demand too much. He had come into contact very nearly with great power, and must be restrained in the drawing on that power, or the fight he had still to fight would not be then his own.

Now, I see in your mind a question as to the possibility of demanding unwisely from us and thus obtaining. Things are so ordered that not alone is this possible but continually is it done. Strange as it may seem to you, help is often demanded from these spheres in such a way that it must be given, and yet it were, time and again, better that the asker's own resources should have been employed, and he thereby have risen to greater strength than by this the other way. If a name be called with vehemence by those on earth the owner of that name cannot but be notified of it. He attends and acts as possible and best.

I cannot but think that Jacob made a better advance in his contest with Esau, and with his sons and with the famine, and with the many trials he had to meet, by bringing to bear on them his own strength of personality than had he been able continually to call to his aid his Angel-guide to do what he could do himself. This help would be often refused and he, unable to understand, would probably have been hindered in his faith and perplexed. Sometimes the help would have been given, and in so patent a way as to require little aspiration to understand, and so, little advancement.

But I will not pursue this to greater length. My object in citing Jacob's case was to show you that you are not farther from us, nor we from you, because you do not see us nor hear our voices. We speak and you hear, but more deeply in yourself than with the outward ear. You do see, but the vision is more inward than that of the outward faculty of sight. And so you should be content; for we are so, and will continue to use you, so you continue in quietness of spirit and in prayer to the Highest through His Son, Whose ministers we are, and in Whose NAME we come.†

Tuesday, November 18, 1913.

When all things visible were created one thing was left not quite complete because the last and greatest of all, and that was man. He was left to develop and, being given to possess great power, he was shown the onward way that he should tread, and left to tread it. But not alone. For all the hierarchy of the heavenly realms were his beholders to see how he would do with those gifts which had been given him.

I do not speak at this time of evolution expressly, as understood by scientists, nor of fall and uprising again, as taught by those who profess theological knowledge, but rather of the broader aspect, as we contemplate man's aspirations and what has come of them. And looking forward, also, it is permitted us to weigh his future, and to see a little way ahead into those long reaches and realms of wide expanse which lie before us all.

Courage in Thinking.

Nor in doing this am I able to constrain myself within the limits of doctrinal theology as understood by you. For it is indeed constrained and straitened so greatly that one who has lived so long in wider room would fear to stretch himself lest he foul his elbows against the confining walls of that narrow channel; and hesitates to go at any pace ahead, obliged as he is to travel, lest worse than this be his lot.

No, my friend, shocking and startling as it be to those whose orthodoxy is as the breath of their body to them, more saddening is it to us to see them so much afraid to use what freedom of will and reason they have lest they go astray, mistaking rigid obedience to code and table for loyalty to Him Whose Truth is free.

Think you for a moment. What manner of Master-Friend is He to them who tremble so at His displeasure? Is it that He is waiting and watching, with sinister smile, to catch them in His net who dare to think and think in error sincerely? Or is this He Who said, "Because you are lukewarm, and neither cold nor hot, I will reject you"? Move and live and use what powers are given prayerfully and reverently and then, if you do chance to err, it will not be of obduracy and wilfulness but of good intent. Shoot with strong arm and feet well and firmly set, and if you miss the mark by once or by twice, your feet shall still be firm and the word "Well done!" for you shot amiss, yet in His good service, and as you were able to do, so you did. Be not afraid. It is not those who strike and shoot and sometimes miss the mark whom He rejects, but the craven who fear to fight for Him at all. This I say boldly for I know it is true, having seen the outcome of both manner of lives when those who have lived them issue forth among us here, and seek their proper place and the gate by which they may pass onward this way.

And now, my ward and fellow-servant in the Army of the Lord, listen well awhile, for I have that to say which may be not very familiar to your way of thinking, and I would that you record it aright.

The Divinity of the Christ.

Many there are among you who do not find it in them to accept the Christ as God. Now, there is much light talk of this matter on both sides of the Veil. For not with you on earth alone but also here we have to seek in order to know, and miracles of revelation are not thrust upon us; nor is our own freedom of reasoning constrained by any higher power than our own. Guided we are, as you are, too, but not forced to believe this or that in any of the many ways in which this might be done. So there are here, also, many who say that Christ is not God, and so saying think they have made an end of the matter.

It is not my present purpose to prove to you the contrary and positive truth, nor even to state that truth affirmatively. It is rather that I would endeavour to show you and them what manner of question this is, and how it is not conducive to an understanding of it, by even the little we may, to speak in terms without first defining them.

First, then, what is meant by God? Do they mean a localized personality when they think of the Father—a person such as a man is? If so it is obvious that the Christ is not He, or this would create a double person or two personalities in one in such a way that distinction of each would be impossible. It is not that way the Oneness of which He spoke is to be sought. Two equal Persons united is an unthinkable condition, and one which reason rejects at once.

Or is it meant that He is the Father in manifestation as Man? So, then, are you and so am I His servants. For the Father is in all of us.

Or is it that in Him was the fullness of the Father, undivided? So in you and in me also dwells the Father, for Him it is not possible to divide.

Yet if it be said that the Whole of the Father dwells in Him but not in us, I say that is an opinion and no more, and also an illogical one; for if the Father as a Whole dwells in the Christ, then either the Christ is the Father without distinction, and none else, or the Whole Father dwelling in the Christ must cease to dwell in Himself of necessity. This also is not reason.

So it is first necessary that we understand that the Father is the Name we give to the highest aspect of God we are able to

Life Beyond the Veil

think of. And even this we do not understand, for it is frankly confessed that He is beyond our understanding.

I cannot define Him to you, for I have not seen Him Who to all less than Himself is not visible entirely. What I have seen is a Manifestation of Him in Presence Form, and that is the highest I have attained previously.[13]

Then the Christ in His Unity with the Father must be also above us as to our understanding, as He is above us in Himself. He tells us so much as we are able to think of, but not to understand very much. He manifested the Father, and such qualities of the Holy Supreme as were capable of manifestation in the body to us. Little more we know, but grow in knowledge as we grow in humility and reverential love.

As He is One with the Father, so we are One with Him. And we dwell in the Father by our dwelling in Him Who is the blending of what we call the Human and the Divine. The Father is greater than He, as He Himself once said. By how much greater He did not say, and we could not have understood had He told us.

It may be said by those who read this that I have cut away the scaffolding and left no building within. My purpose, friend, I stated at the first. It was not now to rear a building, but rather to point out that the first thing to build is a sure foundation; and that any structure raised on one not sure must, now or later, fall, and much labour be in vain. And this indeed have men been doing more than they realize; and that is why so much is misty when it might be plain to view. Not all, of course, but enough to make the road much brighter than it is.

I speak not so much to instruct, in this present message, but rather to give men pause. For ratiocination (judgement based on logic) may be fascinating to certain minds, but is not meat for the soldier. It flatters with its perfect logic and well-balanced

---

[13] This would appear to indicate that Zabdiel is claiming he has witnessed an image of the First Source and Centre in Presence Form. That very much surprises me, as both the Urantia Book and the Padgett Messages indicate one must reach Paradise for one to be in the presence of, and see in a spiritual sense only, Father. And Zabdiel is a very long way from that level. However I entirely accept the statement that to see the Son is to see the Father and Jesus certainly reaches out to all of us. G.J.C.

argument, but is not durable to withstand the wear and tear of the wide elements of the spheres. It is not always so wise to affirm, as to say, "I do not know this—yet." Pride often blinds one to the beauty of a humble mind; and it is not true that he who answers a deep problem off-hand is a fountain of wisdom; for assurance is sometimes nearly akin to arrogance, and arrogance is no way true or lovely.

You and I, my friend and ward, are One in Him Whose Life is our assurance of Life continued. In Him we meet and bless each other, as I bless you now, and thank you for your kindly thoughts towards me. †

Wednesday, November 19, 1913.

Love and its Opposite.

And so, dear friend and ward, my words to you are such as many will not receive; yet know this, that many shall come from east and west and sit down at the Feast of the Christ who without knowing Him as to His Natural Divinity, yet love Him for His human kindness and love; for that, at least, they all can understand. And none can comprehend the other His aspect in the fullness of its meaning. And so let us think of other things, and first the relation men incarnate should foster towards Him if they would progress in the way He showed them.

Foremost must they love. That is the first commandment of all, and the greatest. And hard have men found it to keep. They all agree that to love one another is good; and when they come to translate the sentiment into action, how sadly do they fail. And yet, without love nothing in the entire universe would stand, but fall into decay and dissolution. It is the love of God which energizes through all that is; and we can see that love, if we look for it, everywhere. The best way to understand many things is to contrast them with their opposites. The opposite of love is dissolution; because that comes of refraining from the exertion to love. Hatred is also of the opposite, and yet not the essence of it; because hatred of one person is often a mistaken method of expressing love to another.

And what is said of persons is also true of doctrines and aims. Many express their devotion to one cause by their hatred of another. It is foolish and faulty, but not altogether of evil. When a man hates another man, however, he is likely to cease to love more and more until it becomes an effort to love anything at all.

This is one of those things which make for difficulty in this life of the spheres. For not until a man has learned to love all without hating any is he able to progress in this land where love means light, and those who do not love move in dim places where they lose their way, and often become so dull in mind and heart that their perception of the truth is as vague as that of outward things.[14]

There are, on the other part, mansions here which sparkle with light in every stone, and send forth radiance over the country round to a great distance by reason of the high purity in love of those who dwell in them.

Will you describe such a residence as this, and those who live in it? It would help more than this general description, I think.

It is not easy, as you will know one day. And if I accede to your request, you will understand the result will not be true to fact, inasmuch as it will be inadequate. Nevertheless, I will do as you desire. What residence particularly would you wish me to describe?

Tell me of your own, please.

In the Tenth Sphere are conditions which do not obtain in those of lower degree, least of all in your own sphere of earth.

---

[14] This is precisely why the fear that surrounds spirit communication in Christian circles is so misplaced. Yes there are dark and also misleading spirits. But the darker they are the less knowledge they have, and the only thing that one should be on guard against, is any spirit that does not act in love, and with full regard for the free will of the human. It is totally impossible for a dark malicious spirit to successfully impersonate a spirit of high standing. With a little bit of discernment one can soon discover how advanced a spirit is. However I will concede that one has to take mediumship very seriously to ensure you do not **attach** a dark spirit to yourself. This is a totally different subject beyond the scope of this book. But acting exactly as the Rev. Vale Owen has, and by approaching this matter in prayer and with request for protection and to receive only Truth, will ensure that his own spirit guardians protect him, as they did. G.J.C.

"Now we see Through a Glass Darkly."

If it were possible that I should take you now into that sphere you would not see anything at all, because your condition is not yet fitted to it. What you would see would be a mist of light, more or less intense according to what region of that sphere you were in. In the lower spheres you would see more, but not all, and what you were able to see you would not understand in every part.

Suppose you take a fish out of the water and put him in a globe and take him through a town, how, much, think you, would he firstly see, and secondly understand? I think he would see some few inches beyond the circumference of his habitat—the water, which is his natural environment. Put your face where he can see you, and then your hand instead. What would he know of these things?

So would you be in these spheres; and only by training would you be able to energize and use your faculties therein with ease and profit. Now further, how would you, in the language of the fishes, describe to them the Abbey of Westminster, or even your own village church? If that fish were to make known to you how unreasonable you were when you told him you were hindered by his own limitations; or if he told you that he did not believe there was such a place as the church or Abbey, which you named but could not describe to him, how would you convince him that the unreason was of his own, and not of your, making?

Zabdiel's Heavenly Home.

Still, since you wish it, I will tell you what I can of my own house and home; and you will probably think I might have done better when I finish, and best of all had I refrained altogether.

The country in which we built our house touches many spheres, and among them those whose natures radiate many colours according to their virtues, and which coincide most nearly with those of the people with whom I dwell. These colours are mostly other than those you know, but all those you know are here, and in almost infinite combination and hue. According to the occupation in which we are mentally engaged at any time the blend of colours varies, and the atmosphere takes on that tint.

Life Beyond the Veil

Then the house also vibrates and responds to the thoughts and aspirations, whether of prayer sent onwards, or help willed backward through the spheres behind us, in which direction lies the earth plane.

Music also proceeds from us, not necessarily by mouth, but more often directly from the heart; and this is taken up also in response by the buildings around us, which are part of our energizing; and also the trees and flowers and all plant life is affected and responds. Thus colour and music are not merely inanimate here, but filled with our life, and vibrate to our will.

The house is square, and yet the walls are not four alone, nor at angles each to the others. They, too, are blended, and the outer and inner atmosphere mingles through them. These walls are not for our protection, but for other uses, and one is to concentrate our vibrations, to focus them in their transmission to distant regions where our help is needed and desired. Thus we reach the earth also and sense your doings there, and send you words of instruction, or help in other forms, in answer to the prayers which come to us for us to deal with.

Here also descend those of higher spheres and, by means of these houses and other influences prepared, become tangible to us that we may commune with them on matters which perplex us.

From this house also we send such strength to those who from time to time are commissioned to us from the lower spheres as enables them, for the period of their sojourn among us, to endure the conditions of this sphere with no great discomfort; and also to converse with and to see and hear us, which otherwise they might not do.

As to the aspect of this house from outside, I will give you the description of one of those of a lower sphere which is nearer your own. He told me that when he came in sight of it he was reminded of the words, "a city which is set on a hill whose light cannot be hid." He was a long distance away, but paused and descended to the ground to rest (for he came so far by aerial travel). He shaded his eyes, and gradually was able to look again at the mansion on the hill, far away, in its brightness.

He said he saw the great towers; but they shone so brightly with their blue light that he could not tell where they actually ended, because the light shot up into the heavens above and seemed to continue there indefinitely. Then the domes—some were red and some gold, and the light from these was likewise too dazzling to see where they ended, or what was their size. The gates and walls likewise shone silver and blue and red and violet, and blazed with dazzling light which bathed the hill below, and the foliage of the trees around, and he wondered how he would enter and not be consumed.

But we saw him, and sent messengers to deal with his difficulty; and when at last he turned to bless us and depart, his mission being ended, he said to us, "A thought strikes upon me at this time of parting. My fellow-workers will ask me what manner of place is that to which I have been; and how shall I tell them of this glory when once again I am altogether of my own sphere, and resume its more straitened powers?"

And we replied, "Son, you will never quite be as you were, hereafter. For in you will remain somewhat of this sphere's light and perception. But what you in your heart are able to remember will be of larger measure than you can give to them. For they would not understand if you could tell them; and to tell them you would perforce have to use the language which is current here. Therefore tell them to bend their wills to further development, and one day they shall come and see for themselves what you have seen but are unable to relate."

And so he went away in great joy uplifted. This be your own also, friend, and the words we gave him now I give to you. †

Chapter 3

The Earthly and the Heavenly

Recurring science—Tales of faerie and magic—The passing of materialism—The inter-relation of spheres—Purified by suffering—Origin of species—Man's place in the universe.

Friday, November 21, 1913.

Not everyone who runs reads aright, for they who run are sometimes of too impatient a mind in regard to those things which are not of apparent importance, and only the apparent is of importance to such as these. And so it comes to pass that much that is written very plainly is no word to them, and its message of significance is left unheeded.

This is so in the various signs which are written in what men term nature; that is, the surface phenomena of spirit power energizing in and through matter. Thus it is also in the movement of peoples and nations, as they work out their destiny according to their own proper and peculiar characters.

And thus it is, in perhaps a less degree, in the discoveries of science, as popularly understood. Let us for a short while consider this last and see if there is any message to those who would search more deeply than most, who have time to run only and not to read.

Recurring Science.

Science, as history, repeats itself, but never in exact duplicate. Broad principles govern, from time to time, the search for knowledge, and are succeeded by others in their turn which, having served, then also fall behind into a secondary place in order that other principles may receive the more concentrated and undivided attention of the race. But from time to time, as the ages go by, these principles return again—not in the same order of sequence—to receive the attention of a new race. And so the march of human progress goes on.

Items of discovery also are lost and found anew, often in other than their original guise, and with some strange features added, and other old features lacking.

In order to make what is here set down more plain, I will come to details by way of example.

There was a time when science did not mean what it means to men to-day: when there was a soul in science and the outer manifestation in matter was of secondary interest. Thus it was with alchemy, astrology, and even engineering. It was known in those days that the world was ruled from many spheres, and ministered to by countless hosts of servants, acting freely of their own will but within certain strait limits laid down by those of greater power and higher authority. And men in those days studied to find out the different grades and degrees of those spiritual workers, and the manner of their service in the different departments of nature and of human life, and the amount of power exercised by each several class.

And they found out a considerable number of facts, and classified them. But inasmuch as these facts, laws and regulations and conditions were not of the earth sphere but of the spiritual, they were obliged to express them in a language apart from that of common use.

When another generation grew up whose energies, were directed in other ways, these, not considering well what manner of knowledge was contained in the lore of their ancestors, said the language was allegorical, or symbolic; and thus doing they also made the facts themselves assume a shadowy form, until at last there was little of reality left.

Tales of Faerie and Magic.

Thus it happened with regard to the study of the spiritual powers of varying degree and race, and this issued in the fairy tales of Europe and the magic stories of the East. These are really the surviving lineal and legitimate descendants of the science of the past, added to, subtracted from, and distorted in many ways. And yet if you study to read these tales in the light of what I have said, you will see that, when you have separated the essentials from the more modern embroidering, there are to be found there embedded, like the cities of Egypt under the sands of the ages, solid facts of science or knowledge as spiritually considered.

Would you, please, give a specific instance, by way of illustration?

There is the story of Jack and the Beanstalk. In the first place, look at the name. Jack is colloquial for John, and the original John was he who wrote the Book of the Revelation. The Beanstalk is an adaptation of Jacob's Ladder, by which the upper, or spiritual, spheres were reached. Those spheres once attained, are found to be real countries and regions, with natural scenery, houses and treasures. But these are sometimes held by guardians not altogether in amity with the human race who, nevertheless, by boldness and skill of mind are able to wrest those treasures away and return to earth with them. And also they are able, by natural quickness of character, to prevent those guardians from regaining possession of these treasures of wisdom and depriving the human race of the right won by the conquest of the bolder sort.

Now, this is picturesque, and is made to assume a quaint and even ludicrous guise by reason of its being handed down from age to age by those who did not understand its deeper import. Had they done so most certainly they had not nicknamed the original as Jack. But, as his customary attire of dress will show you, this came about in an age when things holy and spiritual were had in light esteem by reason of the inability of men to realize the actual presence of spiritual beings among them. So, also, they garbed a demon, and gave him spiked ears and a tail, and for a similar reason—that his actuality to them was mythical. The personality they made of him was mythical indeed.

The story I have named is one of many. Punch and Judy might represent the transactions in which the two who stood out most reprobate were Pilate and Iscariot. And from the manner in which these solemn, and indeed awful, incidents are related, the levity of the age in such matters is apparent.

Well, so it is, and has been ever. But now, to-day, the spiritual is returning among men to claim a place, if not adequate to its importance, at least of greater consideration than of these last centuries.

The Passing of Materialism.

Thus, in other guise outwardly, but inwardly more akin, the

broad principle which governed the Egyptian astrologers, and the wisdom which Moses learned and used to such effect, is returning to-day to lift men up a little higher and to put a meaning into that dead materialism of the past which, handling things produced of the energizing of life-shells, bones and fossil stones—denied the Author of Life His place in life's grand arena. It spoke of the orderly working of natural law—and denied the One Source of all order and all working. It spoke of beauty—and forgot that beauty is not unless the spirit of man perceives it, and that spirit is because He Who is Spirit is forever.

We are watching, and we are guiding as we may and opportunity is given us. If men respond to our prompting there is an age to come more full of light and the beauty of love and life than that just passing away. And I think they will respond, for the new is better than the old, and from behind us we feel the pressing of those of higher wisdom and power as we look earthward. And so we do what we are impressed is their intention and desire.

We are not given to be able to see very far ahead. That is a special study, and it is not of the duties of the band of workers to which I am attached. But we are glad to find our endeavours in many hearts meet with ready response, and we hope for greater opportunity, as years go by, to show men how near we are to them, and how great they are potentially if they but be humble in spirit, and quiet, and strive after holiness and purity in thought and desire, looking to Him, the Example of man at his greatest, and seeking to reproduce in themselves that beauty of holiness they may read, even as they run; for a glance at that One His Life should entrance one who has in himself to see what beauty is. For Him we love, and to Him we do reverence, Whose peace be to you in all things, all your days, dear friend. Amen. †

Monday, November 24, 1913.

The Inter-Relation of the Spheres.

Moreover, friend, it is a good thing and a helpful to bear in mind our presence at all times; for we are near, and that in ways both many and various. When we are personally near at hand we are able to impress you with helpful thoughts and intuitions, and so to order events that your work may be facilitated and your way more clear than otherwise it would appear to you.

When in person we are in our own spheres, we still have means whereby we are informed not alone of what has happened in and around you, but also what is about to happen, if the composition of circumstances pursue its normal course.

Thus preserving contact with you, we maintain and ensure our guardianship that it be continuous and unceasing, and our watchfulness that it shall in no way fail on your behalf. For here, and through the spheres between us and you, are contrivances by which intelligence is sent on from one sphere to those beyond and, when necessity require it, we enjoin others to carry out some mission to you, or, if the occasion so requires, we come to earth ourselves, as I have done at this time.

But further still, and in addition to this, we are able each to come into contact with his own charge direct in certain ways, and to influence events from our own place. Thus you will understand that the whole economy of the Creator, through its manifold spheres of light, is unified in action and correlated. So that no part is but is influenced by all those other parts, and what you do on earth not only is registered in the heavens, but has effect on our minds and thoughts, and so on our lives.

Be, therefore, of very careful mind and will; for your doings in thought and your doings in word and your doings in act are all of great import, not alone to those you see and touch around you, but also to those around you unseen and untouched by you, but who see and touch you constantly and often. Not these alone, but those who go about their business in their own spheres are so affected. It is so in my own, I know, and how much higher I do not hazard to say. But, were you to ask me, I would reply that your doings are multiplied by transmission through the spheres of light by seventy times seven; and that no end is found to their journey within the ken of man or angel. For I little doubt, if that at all, they find out at last the very Heart of God.

Be ye, therefore, perfect, because your Father Who is in the Heaven of the Heavens is perfect; and no imperfect thing can find acceptance and approval to enter where He is in His awe-inspiring Beauty.

Highlands of Heaven

And what, then, of those spheres where they who do not love good and beauty dwell? Well, we are also in touch with those, and the help sent there is as readily sent as to the earth sphere; for those realms of darkness are but further removed, and not disconnected, from us. Those who are there are learning their lesson as are you in your earth sphere, but theirs is dimmer than yours—no more than this. For still are they sons and daughters of the One All Father, and so our brothers and sisters too. And these we help when they cry, as we help you at your petition. It has been given you already to know somewhat of the conditions of life there obtaining. But what your mother wrote I may here supplement a little.[15]

Purified by Suffering.

Light and darkness are states of the spirit, as you know. When those dwelling in the darkness cry for light that means that they are become out of touch with their environment. So we send them what help is needed; and that is usually direction by which they find their way—not into regions of light, where they would be in torture, and utterly blinded, but—into a region less dark, and tinctured by just so much of light as they may bear until they outgrow that state and cry in their longing for more.

When a spirit leaves a dark region for one less dark he experiences an immediate sense of relief and comfort by comparison with his former state. For now his environment is in harmony with his own inner state of development. But as he continues to develop in aspiration after good, he gradually becomes out of harmony with his surroundings, and then, in ratio to his progress, so his discomfort increases until it becomes not less than agony. Then in his helplessness, and approaching near to despair, having come to that pass when his own endeavours can go no further, he cries for help to those who are able to give it in God's Name, and they enable him one stage onward nearer to the region where dimness, rather than darkness, reigns. And so he at last comes to the place where light is seen to be light; and his

---

[15] Referring to the messages in Vol. 1 of The Life Beyond the Veil—The Lowlands of Heaven, chap. 3.

Life Beyond the Veil

onward way is henceforth not through pain and anguish, but from joy to greater joy, and hence to glory and glory greater still.

But oh, the long, long ages some do take until they come into that light, ages of anguish and bitterness; and know all the time that they may not come to their friends who wait them until their own unfitness is done away; and that those great regions of darkness and lovelessness must first be trod.[16] But do not mistake my words of their meaning. This is no vengeance of an angry God, my ward and friend. God is our Father; and He is Love. All this sorrow is of necessity, and is ordered by those laws which govern the sowing, and the reaping of that which is sown. Even here, in my own place, where many things both wonderful and lovely we have learned, yet not yet have we attained to plumb and sound this mystery to its lowest depth. We do understand, as we were unable when in the earth life, that it is of love that these things are ordained. I say we are able to understand where formerly we were able but to say we trusted and believed. Yet little more of this awe-inspiring mystery do we know; and are content to wait until it is made more plain to us. For we know enough to be able to believe that all is wise and good; as those in those dark hells will know one day. And this is our comfort that they will and must be drawn onward and upward into this great and beautiful universe of light, and that then they will confess, not only that what is is just, but that it is of love and wisdom too, and be content.

Such have I known, and do know, and am of their number in the service of the Father. And it seems to me their praise and blessing of Him are no way lacking in love in comparison of ours who have not journeyed through those awful depths. Nay, friend, for I will confess to you this one thing else: that sometimes, as we have paid our united worship together prostrate before the Light of the Throne of the Heavens, I have felt that there is something in their worship lacking in mine; and have almost half-wished that I might have that in me too.[17]

---

[16] The Padgett Messages, referred to in the recommended reading, indicate that about the time this book was being received, Julius Caesar was still deep in the hells - over 2000 years later.

[17] This is probably the only reference I have found in any of these volumes to a deep Spiritual Truth that to be honest I expected to find expounded here. And that is the difference between intellectual prayer

39

Highlands of Heaven

Yet this would not be right; and doubtless the Father takes, in His Love, what is in us to give Him.[18] Nevertheless, it is very sweet, that saying of the Master, and rings true here where love is seen in the beauty of its nakedness: Because she is forgiven much, therefore she loves the more.

God keep you in His Love, my friend and ward, and nought else matters so you do respond to His sweet caress, and rest in Him. Amen. †

Tuesday, November 25, 1913

If it were but a little of faith a man should have in him he would be able to understand what I have written by your mind and hand. But not to many is it given to see into the truth of things, and to know them as true indeed. So has it been down the ages, friend, and so will it be yet for ages many. So far it is given to see, but yet we look forward and onward still, and ahead we think we see a world of men moving and doing in a greater light than that which is about them to-day; and in that day they will see and understand how near are we to them, not in books alone, but in the daily lives they lead. Meanwhile we do our part, ever watchful, ever hopeful and, if our joy is sometimes mingled with a sadness we cannot altogether put away while men and we do not go hand

---

and soul-based prayer. It's a subject that is nearly impossible to communicate to those who are highly intellectual in nature, as they just can't get the difference, or the reality of heart centred prayer. But if you manage it, you will know the difference. Sometimes in Christian circles those who have achieved this, call it feeling the presence of the Holy Spirit, and in that they are correct. G.J.C.

[18] Following on from the point above, this is another massive Spiritual Truth, and the Urantia Book has a fabulous quote on this, which I will repeat here: Mortal man cannot possibly know the infinitude of the heavenly Father. Finite mind cannot think through such an absolute truth or fact. But this same finite human being can actually feel--literally experience--the full and undiminished impact of such an infinite Father's LOVE. Such a love can be truly experienced, albeit while quality of experience is unlimited, quantity of such an experience is strictly limited by the human capacity for spiritual receptivity and by the associated capacity to love the Father in return. (Paper 3 - The Attributes of God, (50.4) 3:4.6) G.J.C.

in hand, as is our wish, still, again, we know that we are coming nearer together; and all is well.

And now to our present task, my ward; for while it is day I would that we work together; for when the night descends then you will find another Day, but not as now; and other opportunities of service, but not such as these. So let us do what we can while we have command of these present conditions, and we shall do better work when wider spheres are opened to us,—both to you and me.

Science, as you know it, is not coterminous (having the same meaning or boundaries) with what you know, for we look deeper into those fundamentals which are of spiritual origin; and worldly science is but now beginning to admit this truth into her councils. Thus we are already drawing nearer each to other; or rather it would be more true to say that those among you who are searching into the meaning of the phenomena of your sphere are coming nearer to us as we draw them upward to higher and deeper searching.

For this we are thankful, and it emboldens us to continue in the same path; and this we do in sure faith that men will continue to follow where we lead, so we be careful to lead them wisely and well.

The Origin of Species.

I now would tell you somewhat of the inner meaning of what men call the origin of species in animal life. But now, and at once, I would say the term is all too large; for the origin of the different creations in animal life is not found in the realm of matter, but has its genesis in these realms. We have learned here that, when the Universe of systems was moving towards its present form and constitution, those who had charge to watch and work took their counsels from those of higher degree, and on those counsels shaped their own wisdom.

At that time it was seen that in the heavenly spheres there were many diversities both of the forms of life as bodily manifest, and of mind in its working. And it was resolved that the universe was meant to reflect the personalities and types of those who were commissioned to carry out the work of its development. To this conclusion they were divinely guided, for when their plan was completed it was given them by revelation to know that the Divine approval was upon it in general kind; but that it was not of absolute perfection. Nevertheless, it received the imprimatur of the All Father Who graciously granted them freedom to work out His will according to their own capacities and powers.

Thus arose the different orders and species of animal and vegetable and mineral life, and also of human type and racial character. And these things being initiated, again the Divine Mind pronounced His general approval or, as our Bible has it, He found it to be "very good."

But high as were those who were chief in this matter of creation, yet they were less than the Only Omnipotent and, as the work of ordering the universe was very great, and wide in extent, the imperfections of their work became magnified as they worked out; so that, to a single mind, and one of low degree, as is that of a man, those imperfections loomed vast and great. For it is not competent to one who is so small and undeveloped to be able to see both good and evil equally, but the evil is the easier seen by him, and the good too high and wonderful for him to grasp its meaning and power.

Man's Place in the Universe.

But if men would keep in mind one thing, they would find the existence of this imperfection, mingled with so much more that is wonderful and wise, the easier to understand. That one thing is this: that the Universe was not created for him alone, any more than the sea was created alone for the use of the sea-animals that dwell therein, or the air for the birds. Man invades both sea and air and calls them of his kingdom to conquer and to use. And he is right. They do not belong to the fish and the birds. The dominion is to the greater being, and that being is man. He is lord by permission, and rules the earth in which, and over which, his Maker has placed him.

But there are greater than he and, as he rules the lesser and uses them for the development of his faculties and personality, so these rule him and use him likewise.

And this is just and wise, for these Angels and Archangels and Princes and Powers of God are His servants also, and their development and training are necessary as that of men. But by how much these are greater than he, respectively, so must the means and material of their training be of higher nature and sublimity than those which are given him to use. According to the innate power of any being, man or angel, so is his environment proportioned and constituted.

Let men remember this and keep it in mind, and then they will the better appreciate the dower (estate legacy) of freewill given to them, a gift which no one of all the heavenly hierarchy may take from him. And they would not if they might; for in so doing their material would be deteriorated in quality, and the less capable of enabling them in their own advancement.

Now, I fear that some who read what I have written will say that hereby man becomes merely the tool of those of higher grade, to do with him what they will for their own advantage. Not so; and for the reason I have just stated—that he is, and ever must remain, a freewill being.

But more, the one great power which animates those who serve the Father here is Love. These are no mere despots of oppression. Power and oppression are mutually exclusive of earth creation. Here power means an issuing forth of love, and the greater the power the greater the love which is sent forth.

And this, moreover. Let those whose fight with evil is fierce and dire remember and realize well the privilege and high destiny which is theirs to attain. For in this is a warrant and sure token that man has been permitted into the Council and work of those of very high degree, to join with them in this great task of working out salvation for the whole universe on the lines laid down so long ago. And this task is one which a man with courage will grapple with full eagerly, for it is he who will understand so much as this: that what angels and Princes of high estate are doing he is doing with them in his own sphere and degree and, knowing this, he will rejoice and be strong.

Seeing also that his work is one with our own, and ours is his, and with only one object set before us both, which is the betterment of all life and all things, he will know that our strength is at his call, so he call wisely and with due humility and simple trust. For so we delight to help men, who are our comrades in this fight, and our fellow-workers in the one great field of the Universe of God.

Highlands of Heaven

We see more than you do of the awful painful effort of those who err from this service, and yet we do not despair, because we see also the more clearly the meaning and purpose of it all. And thus seeing, we know that men will one day rejoice as we do when they too shall, each in his own time, ascend to the higher spheres of service and, from this point of vantage, continue his development. In that day he too will use for his training the material we are using, and of which he is a part and portion, when others have taken his place, and he the place of those who now are lifting him upward.

"To him that overcometh," said the Christ, "will I give to sit with Me in My Throne, even as I overcame, and am set down with My Father in His Throne." To the strong is the Kingdom, my dear charge and ward, and to the one who has shall be given.

This much now, and I must cease for this time. But the matter is much greater than I have been able to tell in this short message. If God permit I will tell you more anon.

And now, do well and you shall fare well: and if you be strong, then out of your strength shall sweetness come. For so it is in these realms that they are most sweet and lovely whose strength is greatest. This remember, and it shall solve many problems which perplex men much. God's light be with and around you always, and you shall not stumble then. †

Chapter 4

Earth the Vestibule of Heaven

Inspiration—Like attracts like—The squire and his wife—Our spiritual status—The man who thought he knew—The penalty of spiritual blindness.

Wednesday, November 26, 1913.

Many things there are of which I might speak to you, matters of organization, and of the exercise of power as its influence and effect are seen by us as it passes on its way through our spheres to that of earth. Some of these things you would not be able to understand, and others, perhaps, but few among you would believe if they understood them. So I confine myself to the simpler principles and the mode of their working; and one of these is the modus operandi of the connexion obtaining between us and you in the matter of inspiration.

Inspiration.

Now, this is a word very expressive if understood aright; and very misleading if not so understood. For that we inbreathe into the hearts of men knowledge of the truth of God is true. But it is only a very little of the truth. For more than this we do give to them and, with other things, strength to progress and to work God's will, love to work that will from high motive, and wisdom (which is knowledge blended with love) to work God's will aright. And if a man be said to be inspired, this is not a singular case, nor one exceptional. For all who try to live well, and few do not in some degree, are by us inspired, and so helped.

But the act of inbreathing is not a very accurate way of describing the method of our work. It would the better apply as used subjectively of the one so-called inspired. He breathes in our waves of vibrating energy as we direct those waves to him. So a man breathes in and fills his lungs of the fresh breeze on the hill-side, and is refreshed. Even so he breathes in the refreshing streams of power we waft towards him.

Highlands of Heaven

But we would not limit the meaning of the word to those alone who in elegant words tell out to the world some new truth of God, or some old truth refurbished and made as new. The mother tending her child in sickness, the driver of the engine along the railway, the navigator guiding the ship, all, and others, do their work of their peculiar powers self-contained, but, as occasion and circumstances require, modified and supplemented by our own. This is so even when the receiver of our help is unaware of our presence; and this more often than not. We give gladly while we are able; and we are able so long as no barrier is opposed to us by him we would help.

This barrier may be raised in many ways. If he be of obstinate mind, then we may not impose on him our counsel; for he is free to will and to do. And sometimes when we see great need of our help being given, the barrier of sin is interposed and we cannot get through it. Then those who counsel wrongly (Reference to dark spirits who can get through and or misguided humans) do their work, and grievous is the plight of those to whom they minister.

Each man, and every woman too, chooses his own companions wittingly or unwittingly. If he mock the idea that we are present in the earth sphere, or that any influence may proceed from what to him is the unseen and unknown, that matters not so he be of good intent and right motive. He offers to us no barrier of absolute negation. We help him gladly, for he is honest, and will some day in his honesty own his error—someday soon. Only this that he is not then so sensitive to catch our meaning; and he will often mistake us, not knowing what we would impress upon his mind.

If the water-wheel be well oiled on its axle, then the water turns it easily; but if it be rusty, then the force must be increased in volume, and the wear, both of the wheel and its axle, is greater, and it moves more heavily. Also, the sailors may be accurate in obeying the instructions of the captain, even if he were totally strange to them. But if he be known to them well, then they are the better able in the storm, of a dark night, to catch his meaning in the orders he gives, for they know his mind and need little words and few to tell them of his wishes. So they who know us more naturally and more intimately than others are in better fettle to receive our words.

Inspiration, therefore, is of wide meaning and extent in practice. The prophets of old time—and those of to-day—received our instruction according to the quickening of their faculties. Some were able to hear our words, some to see us—both as to their spiritual bodies—others were impressed mentally. These and other ways we employ, and all to one end, namely: to impart through them to their fellow-men instruction as to the way they should go, and in what way they should order their lives to please God, as we are able to understand His will from this higher plane. Our counsel is not of perfection, nor infallible. But it never leads astray those who seek worthily and with much prayer, and with great love. These are God's own, and they are a great joy to us their fellow-servants. Nor need we go far afield to find them, for there is more good in the world than evil, and, as in each good and evil is proportioned, so are we able to help, and so is our ability limited.

So do both of these two things—see that your light is kept burning as they who wait for their Lord, for it is His will we do in this matter, and it is His strength we bring. Prayers are allotted us to answer and His answer is sent by us His servants. So be watchful and wakeful for our coming, who are of those who came to Him in the Wilderness, and in Gethsemane (albeit I think they would be of much higher degree than I).

And the other to bear in your mind is this: See you keep your motive high and noble, and seek not selfishly, but for others' welfare. We minister best to the progress of those who seek our help for the benefit of their brethren rather than their own. In giving we ourselves receive, and so do you. But the larger part of motive must be to give, as He said, and that way the greater blessing lies, and that for all.

Remember His word, "I have power to lay down My life—but I lay it down for My sheep." This He did in very truth, and with no dissembling of motive. Nevertheless, in laying down that life He took life up again more glorious, and that only because His gift was empty of self, and full of love. So do you, and you will find your sweetness in the giving and receiving, both. It is a task most difficult of perfect fulfilment. But it is the right and good way, and must needs be trod. And He has shown us how.

The vessels of the flower empty themselves of their scent to the enjoyment of man, but only to be filled again with more and, so doing, come to more perfect maturity day by day. The word of kindness is returned, and two people made happy by the initial act of one. Kind words later beget kind deeds. And so is love multiplied, and with love, joy and peace. And they who love to give, and give for love's own sake are shooting golden darts which fall into the streets of the Heavenly City, and are gathered up and carefully stored away till they who sent them come and receive their treasure once again with increase. †

Thursday, November 27, 1913.

Like Attracts Like.

Following on what I have given you, I may add that very few there are who realize in any great degree the magnitude of the forces which are ambient around men as they go about their business day by day. These forces are real, nevertheless, and close at hand. Nay, they mingle with your own endeavours, whether you will or no. And these powers are not all good, but some are malicious, and some are in-between, and neither definitely good nor bad.

When I say "powers" and "forces," it is of necessary consequence that personalities be present with them to use them. For know this, not as of formal assent, but consenting thereto ex animo, (from the heart) that you are not alone, and cannot be or act alone, but must act and will and contrive in partnership, and your partners you do elect, whether you do so willingly or no.

So it behooves that all be curious in their selection, and this may be assured by prayer and a right life. Think of God with reverence and awe, and of your fellow-men with reverence and love; and do all things as knowing we watch you and mark down your inner mind with exact precision, and that, as you are and become now, so you will be when you are awakened here; and what things now to you are material and positive and seem very real will then be of another sphere, and your eyes will open on other scenes, and earth be spoken of as that other sphere, and the life of earth as a journey made and finished, and the money and furniture, and the trees in your garden, and all you now seem to own as your peculiar property will not be any more at hand.

Life Beyond the Veil

Then you will be shown what place and treasures and friends you have earned in the school of endeavour just ended and left behind forever. And you will be either full of sorrow and regret, or compassed with joy unspeakable and light and beauty and love, all at your service, and those your friends who have come on before, now eager to show you some of the scenes and beauties of their present home.

Now what, think you, will that man do whose life on earth has been a closed compartment, with no window for outlook into these spiritual realms? He will do as I have seen many do. He will do according as his heart is fashioned. Most such are unready to own their error, for such are usually positive that the opinions built up during a lifetime, and which have served them so well, cannot be so grievously in error. These have much to pass through before the light will serve their atrophied spiritual sight.

But those who have schooled themselves to sit loose to what are counted for riches and pleasures on earth shall find their laps not large enough for the treasures brought by loving hands, nor their eyes so quick as they may catch all the many smiles of welcome and delight at the surprise they show that, after all, the real reality is just begun, and the new is much better than the old.

And now, my ward and friend let me show you a scene which will illustrate what I have written.

The Squire and his Wife.

On a hill-side green and golden, and with the perfume of many flowers hovering about like music kissed by colour, there is an old gabled house with many turrets and windows like those which first in England were filled with glass. Trees and lawns and, down in the hollow, a large lake where birds of many colours, and very beautiful, sport themselves. This is not a scene of your sphere, but one on this side of the Veil. It were of little profit that I argue to show the reasonableness of such things being here. It is so, and that men should doubt that all that is good and beautiful on earth is here with beauty enhanced, and loveliness made more lovely is, on our part, a matter of wonder quite as great.

On one of the towers there stands a woman. She is clad in the colour of her order, and that colour is not one you know on earth; so I cannot give it a name. But I would describe it as golden-purple; and that will, I fear, convey little to you. She looks out towards the horizon far away across the lake, where low-lying hills are touched by the light beyond. She is fair to look upon. Her figure is more perfect and beautiful than that of any woman on earth, and her face more lovely. Her eyes shine out a radiance of lovely violet hue, and on her brow a silver star shines and sparkles as it answers to her thoughts within. This is the jewel of her order. And if beauty were wanted to make her beauty more complete, it is there in just a tinge of wistfulness, which but adds to the peace and joy of her countenance. This is the Lady of the House where live a large number of maidens who are in her charge to do her will and go forth on what mission she desires from time to time. For the House is very spacious.

Now, if you study her face you will see at once that she is there expectant; and presently a light springs up and flashes from her eyes those beautiful violet rays; and from her lips a message goes; and you know that by reason of the flash of light of blue and pink and crimson which darts from beneath her lips and seems to take wing far too quickly for you to follow it across the lake.

Then a boat is seen coming quickly from the right between the trees which grow on its borders, and the oars flash and sparkle, and the spray around the gilded prow is like small spheres of golden glass mingled with emeralds and rubies as it falls behind. The boat comes to the landing-place, and a brilliantly robed throng leap on to the marble steps which lead them up to the green lawn above. One is not so quick, however. His face is suffused with joy, but he seems also full of wonder, and his eyes are not quite used to the quality of the light which bathes all things in a soft shimmering radiance.

Then from the great entrance, and down towards the party, comes the Lady of the House, and pauses a short distance from the party. The new-comer looks on her as she stands there, and utter perplexity is in his gaze, rapt and intent. Then, at last, she addresses him, and in homely words this shining saint of God welcomes her husband, "Well, James, now you have come to me—at last, dear, at last."

But he hesitates. The voice is hers, but different. Moreover, she died an old woman with grey hair, and an invalid. And now she stands before him a lovely woman, not young nor old, but of perfect grace and beauty of eternal youth.

"And I have watched you, dear, and been so near you all the time. And that is past and over now, and your loneliness is gone forever, dear. For now we are together once again, and this is God's Summerland where you and I will never grow old again, and where our boys and Nellie will come when they have finished what is theirs to do in the earth life."

Thus she talked, that he might get his bearings; and this he did at last, and suddenly. He burst into tears of joy, for it came to him that this indeed was his wife and sweetheart; and love overcame his awe. He came forward with his left hand over his eyes, just glancing up now and then, and when he was near she came quickly and took him into her arms and kissed him, and then throwing one arm about his neck, she took his hand in hers and led him up the steps, with slow and gentle dignity, into the House she had prepared for him.

Yes, that House was the heavenly counterpart of their home in Dorset, where they had lived all their married life until she passed hence, and where he had remained to mourn her absence.

This, my ward, I have set down by way of pointing, with homely incident, the fact that the treasures of heaven are not mere words of sentiment, but solid and real and, if you will not overdo the word, material. Houses and friends and pastures and all things dear and beautiful you have on earth are here. Only here they are of more sublime beauty, even as the people of these realms are of a beauty not of earth.

Those two had lived a good life as country squire and wife, both simple and Godfearing, and kindly to the poor and the rich alike. These have their reward here; and that reward is often unexpected in its nature as it was to him.

This meeting I myself witnessed, for I was one of those who brought him on his way to the House, being then of that sphere where this took place.

What sphere was it, please?

The Sixth. And now, friend, I will close, and would I might show you now some of these beauties which are in store for the simple-hearted who do what they can of love, and seek the righteousness of God to please Him rather than the high places among men. These shall shine as the stars and as the sun, and all around them shall take on more loveliness by reason of their presence near. It is written so, and it is true. †

Friday, November 28, 1913.

We will now try to think of that passage where the Christ of God and Saviour of man speaks to His own as being chosen out of the world. Not alone chosen of the world, but taken out of it. If, then, out of the world, in what abode do they dwell?

First it is necessary to understand in what sense our Saviour speaks of the world. The world in this case is the realm where matter is of dominant importance to the mind, and those who count it so are dwelling, as to their spiritual state and spiritual bodies, in another sphere than those who hold the inverse idea, namely, that matter is but the mode of manifestation adopted and used by spiritual beings, and subservient to those who use it, as a workman uses clay or iron.

Our Spiritual Status.

Those who are held to be in the world, therefore, are spiritually in the sphere which is near the earth, and these are sometimes called earthbound spirits.[19] It matters not whether they be clothed with material bodies, or have shed them and stand discarnate; these are bound and chained to the world, and cannot rise into the spheres of light, but have their conversation among those who move in the dim regions about the planet's surface. These, then, are holden of the earth, and are actually within the circumference of the earth sphere.

But He had lifted His chosen out of this sphere into the spheres of light and, although still incarnate, yet as to their spiritual bodies, they were in those higher spheres. And this explains their manner of life and conduct subsequently. It was from these spheres that they drew all that indomitable courage and great joy and fearlessness which enabled them to count the

---

[19] In a short book that I have published called "Getting the Hell Out of Here" this is called the Astral Plane, and it is very well described in only one book that I have discovered, namely that by J.S.M. Ward called "A Subaltern in Spirit Land - a Sequel to Gone West Part One" G.J.C.

world as being not of their necessity, but merely as the field where they must fight their battle, and then go home to their friends awaiting. What is true of them is true to-day.

It is from the spheres of gloom that fear and uncertainty come to so many, for these are the lot of those who dwell therein discarnate, and not quickened so that they may be able to realize their spiritual environment nevertheless; move and energize in it, and receive in themselves those qualities for which they have fitted themselves by their manner of thinking and of life.

So it is scientifically exact to say that a man may be in the world as to his material body, but not of the world as to his spiritual body.

When these two sorts of men come over here they go each to his own proper sphere and, for lack of clarity of reasoning and judgment, many are very much surprised to find themselves allotted to a place of which they had heard with their outer ears, but had not further inquired as to its reality.

Now, in order to make this more clear, which is of the very elements of knowledge to us on this side, I will tell you of an incident of my own knowledge and experience.

The Man who Thought he Knew.

I was once sent to receive a man who required some careful dealing with, for he was one who had many rather decided opinions as to these realms, and whose mind had been filled with ideas of what was right and proper as to the life continued here. I met him as his spirit attendants brought him from the earth region, and led him to the grove of trees where I awaited him. He walked between them and seemed dazed somewhat, as if he sought what he could not find.

I motioned the two to set him to stand alone before me, and they retired some little distance behind him. He could not see me plainly at first; but I concentrated my will upon him, and at last he looked at me searchingly.

Then I said to him, "Sir, you seek what you cannot find, and

Highlands of Heaven

I may help you. First tell me, how long have you been in this country of ours?"

"That," he answered, "I find difficult to say. I had certainly arranged to go abroad, and thought it was into Africa I was going. But I do not find this place in any way what I expected."

"No, for this is not Africa; and from that country you are a long distance away."

"What is the name of this country, then? And what tribe of people are these? They are white, and very handsome, but I never came on any quite like them, even in my reading."

"Well, there you are not quite exact for a scientist such as you are. You have read of these people without realizing that they were anything more than puppets without life and natural qualities. These are those you have read of as saints and angels. And such am I."

"But," he began, and then paused. He did not believe me, and feared to offend, not knowing what consequences should ensue; for he was in a strange country, among strange folk, and without escort.

"Now," I told him, "you have the biggest task before you that you have ever encountered. In all your journeys you have come to no barrier so high and thick as this. For I will be quite plain to you and tell you the truth. You will not believe it. But, believe me, until you do believe it and understand, you will not have peace of mind, nor will you be able to make any progress. What you have before you to do is to take the opinions of a lifetime, turn them upside down and inside out, and own yourself no longer a scholar and great scientist, but the veriest babe in knowledge; and that nearly all you thought worthy of any consideration at all as to this country was either unworthy a thinking being, or absolutely wrong. These are hard words because they are such of necessity. But look well on me, and tell me, if you can read me, whether I be honest and friendly or no."

He looked on me long and very seriously, and said at last, "Though I am altogether at sea as to what you mean, and your words seem to me like those of some misguided enthusiast, yet your face is honest enough, and I think you wish me well. Now, what is it you want me to believe?"

"You have heard of death?"

"Faced it many a time!"

Life Beyond the Veil

"As you are now facing me. And yet you know neither one nor the other. What kind of knowledge call you that which looks on a thing without knowing what it is?"

"If you will be plain, and tell me something I can understand, I may be able to get the hang of things a little better."

"So. Then first of all you are what you would call dead." At this he laughed outright and said, "Who, are you, and what are you trying to do with me? If you are bent on trying to make a fool of me, say so and be done with it, and let me get on my way. Is there any village near at hand where I can get food and shelter while I think over my future course?"

"You do not require food, for you are not hungry. Nor do you require shelter, for you are not bodily tired. Nor do you observe any sign of night at all."

At this he paused once again, and then replied, "You are quite right; I am not hungry. It is strange, but it is quite true; I am not hungry. And this day, certainly, has been the longest on record. I don't understand it all."

And he fell into a reverie again. Then I said, "You are what you would call dead, and this is the spirit land. You have left the earth, and this is the life beyond, which you must now live, and come to understand. Until you grasp this initial truth further help I cannot give you. I leave you to think it over; and when you wish for me, if you should so wish, I will come to you. These two gentlemen who led you here are attendant spirits. You may question them and they will answer. Only, this remember. You shall not be allowed to ridicule what they say, and laugh at them, as you did but now at my words. Only if you be humble and courteous will I allow you their company. You have in you much that is of worth; and you have also, as many more I have met, much vanity and foolishness of mind. This I will not allow you to flaunt in the faces of my friends. So be wise in time and remember. For you are now on the borderland between the spheres of light and those of shade, and it lies in you to be led into the one, or to go, of your own freewill, into the other. May God help you, and that He will if you will."

Then I motioned to the two attendant spirits, and they came and sat down by him; and I left them sitting there together.

What happened? Did he go up or down?

He did not call for me again, and I did not go to him for a

long time. He was very inquisitive, and the two, his companions, helped him in every possible way. But he gradually found the light and atmosphere of the place uncomfortable, and was forced to withdraw to a dimmer region. Here he made a strenuous effort, and the good at length prevailed in him. But it was a fierce and protracted fight, and one of much galling and bitter humiliation. Still, he was a brave soul and won. Then they were called by those to whom he had been committed by them, and led him once again to the brighter country.

There I went to meet him, in that same spot in the grove of trees. He was a much more thoughtful man, and gentler, and less ready to scoff. So I looked on him silently, and he looked on me and knew me, and then bent his head in shame and contrition. He was very sorry that he had laughed at my words.

Then he came forward slowly and knelt before me, and I saw his shoulders shake with sobbing as he hid his face in his hands.

So I blessed him, with my hand upon his head, and spoke words of comfort and left him. It is often thus. †

Monday, December 1, 1913

The Penalty of Spiritual Blindness.

Not to many is it given to see the light amid the darkness, nor to know the darkness for what it is. But that is a state of their own making; for to everyone who would know the truth there is sent out from these spheres such help and enablement as is needed according to his nature and capacity.

This has ever been, and thus it is to-day. For God is One, not alone as to His Nature, but also as to His manifestation in the outer spheres of His Kingdom.

When He sent forth this present universe of matter He endowed His servants with qualities which made them competent to carry out His purpose, giving them liberty within certain bounds, as I have formerly explained. And one of the laws which governed them was that, among all minor and temporal variations and seeming diversity in the operation of the powers which were put into their hands, unity should be the guiding principle of all, and to that end all should tend eventually.

This principle of unity and consistency has ever been before those high Princes and Dominions, and has never been departed from. Neither is it unregarded today. This men forget, and themselves disregard who marvel that we should interest ourselves in you, our brethren less developed, insomuch as to touch you, and to speak to you and guide you personally and by personal contact of our presence.

Also, it is on our part a marvel that men should be found who hesitate on the way, and fear that to speak to us is wrong, and displeasing to Him Who Himself came into the world for this same reason; that He might show how both the spiritual and the material were but two phases of one great Kingdom, and the unity of both together.

Throughout His teaching this is the one great motive, and for this it was that His enemies put Him to death. Had His Kingdom been of this world alone He had not discounted their temporal aspirations, nor their manner of life as to its ease and grandeur. But He showed that the Kingdom was of those higher realms, and that the Church on Earth was but the vestibule to the Presence Chamber. This being so, then the virtues by which nobility should be measured were those which governed rank in these brighter regions, and not the mixed conditions of the lower portion of that Kingdom, as interpreted by the world.

For that they killed Him; and to-day there is remaining too much, as we see it, of their sentiment, both in the Church and in the world outside. And until men do realize our presence, and our right of consideration as fellow-members of this same Kingdom of the Father, and not until this come to pass, shall men make much advance in the discerning between the light and the darkness.

Blind guides there are too many, friend; and they displease us much by their arrogant sniffing at our work and commission. "Had they known they would not have killed Him—the Lord of Glory." No, surely; but they did kill Him nevertheless. Did these present know that we who come to earth on our loving enterprise were angels, they would not have reviled our work of communion and those who rise above the ruck that we may make our whispers heard. No, but they do revile us and those our friends and brethren. And they shall plead their unknowing and their blindness with like effect as those who killed the Master Christ.

Highlands of Heaven

Zabdiel, this is no doubt all quite true and just. But I think you are, perhaps, speaking with some heat. Also, it was St. Peter who pleaded for the Jews, was it not, and not the Jews themselves?

Aye, friend, I do speak with heat somewhat, in indignation. But there is another heat more generous, and that is the heat of love. It is not true to think of us as always placid and unmoved. We sometimes are angry; and our anger is always just, or it would soon be corrected from those who are over us and see with eyes more clear than our own. But we do never avenge ourselves—remember you that, and remember it well. Nevertheless, in justice, and in love of our friends and co-workers on the earth plane, we do mete out punishment, and that of duty, to those who deal with them unkindly. But I see you do not favour me in this. I will defer to your inclination, therefore, and leave this matter for this time. But what I have said is true every small bit, and worthy to ponder well of those whom it shall be seen to touch.

As to that matter of St. Peter's pleading. Yes, so did he. But keep in mind one more thing also. I speak from this side the Veil, and you hear me through it on the earth side. Now, we have here, as you have there, records of history—the history of these realms—which are carefully kept.[20] And from these records we know that in their judgment here those His accusers did plead this blindness, and to little avail. Light was as darkness to them, and darkness to them was as light, because they were themselves of the darkness. They did not know the Light when He came to them, for this same reason. Very well, they were blind and did not know. Now, blindness here in these spheres is not the effect of the shutting off of the outer light, but proceeds from deeper cause. It

---

[20] It is correct that exact records exist, but I have been puzzled when spirits then claim that different things occurred, when it appears that all they need do is check the records. Then I learned that the records are complex, and it's not a simple matter to, for example, inspect what Jesus thought while he was here. You have to be of a certain level of spiritual advancement, possibly even more advanced than he was at that time, which would be an enormous challenge. But probably inspecting what Pontius Pilate thought would present few issues, since he passed into the hells. G.J.C.

is not outward but inward, of the essence of a man's nature. Because, therefore, they were blind, to the place of the blind were they sent; that is, to the regions of gloom and anguish.

This age is one of great activity in these regions of light. Much energy is being directed to the earth in all its parts. There is scarcely a church or creed unstirred. It is the light being directed into the darkness, and it is a matter of very great responsibility to those who are still in training in the earth sphere. Let them be curious and very brave to see and own this light. This is my warning, and I give it with solemn thoughts. For I speak after much experience in this school where we learn much, and more quickly than by the use of a material brain. Let men search humbly and find out the truth of these matters.

For the rest, we do not appeal on bended knee. That let them also keep in mind. We do not proffer gifts as slaves to princes. But we do come and stand by you with gifts which gold of earth cannot buy; and to those who are humble and good and of a pure mind we give these gifts of ability to understand the Truth as it is in Jesus of certain conviction of life beyond and of the joy of it, of fearlessness of disaster here or hereafter, and of companionship and comradeship with angels.

Friend, I leave you now, and beg you bear with me if I have said what you have less willingly recorded than at other times. I have not unwittingly thus impressed you. And at another time I will endeavor to make amends with messages of brighter hue.

Peace and joy be in your heart, my ward. Amen.†

Chapter 5

The Science of the Heavens

Transmission of spiritual power—The relation of Spirit to matter—Consider the Heavens—The web of light—Spiritual reality—The reality of Heaven—The city by the lake—Old comrades meet—The Temple and its Sanctuary.

Tuesday, December 2, 1913.

Dear friend and ward, I will to-night speak to you of certain matters which connect with the question of transmutation of energy. Energy, as I now employ the word, is to be understood as that intermediary which couples up the motion of will with the effect as displayed to the minds of men. We here are trained to this end that we may, by the motion of our wills, transmit, by what we may call vibration, our thoughts through the intervening spheres, or states, into the earth plane. It is this movement in vibration which I call energy.

Now, you must understand that in using earth-phrasing I am employing a medium which is not adequate to express, either exactly or fully, the science of these spheres and realms. It is necessary, therefore, that I qualify my terms, and when I use the term vibration I do not speak merely of oscillation to and fro alone, but of movements which are sometimes elliptical, sometimes spiral, and sometimes a combination of these and other qualities.

Transmission of Spiritual Power.

From this point of view the atomic system of vibration, which has but of late been revealed to men of science, is to us one with the movements of the planets of this solar sphere, and of other systems far away in space. The motion of earth round the sun, and the motion of the molecules of the atom are vibrations. It matters not by what degree you measure them, or what the diameter of their orbit, they are one in kind, and in degree only do they differ each from other.

But transmutation brings into any such system a change of movement, and the quality of movement being changed, there is also, and of necessity, a change of result. Thus we, acting always in perfect obedience to laws laid down by those higher and wiser than ourselves, concentrate our wills on the movement of certain vibrations, which become deflected and transmuted into other qualities of vibrations, and thus change is wrought.

Usually we do this work slowly and gradually, in order to obtain the exact quantity of divergence from the original quality of vibration intended, and not less or more.

It is by this method that we deal with the actions of men, and the course of nature in all its parts. There are manifold classes and companies who have in charge the various departments of creation—mineral, vegetable, animal, human, terrestrial, solar, and stellar. Beyond this, also, the stars are grouped together and dealt with by hierarchies qualified for that great task.

It is by this same method, then, of the transmutation of energy that systems are gradually developed into worlds, and these worlds furnished with form, and then enabled to produce vegetation and animal life. But, this being so, you will note that all life, and all development, is consequent on the operation of spiritual energy obeying the dictates of the will of spiritual beings. This once grasped, blind force disappears, and intention takes its place intention of intelligent and powerful spiritual workers of various grades operating according to certain fixed laws but, within the bounds of those laws, free and mighty.[21]

The Relation of Spirit to Matter.

Moreover, matter itself is the result of the transmutation of spiritual vibrations into those of grosser sort, and these latter are now being analysed by scientists who have come to the

---

[21] It is curious how this section focuses on the creative aspect of evolution, almost to the point of not explaining that all life is evolutionary, even spiritual life. This may be because the Rev. Vale Owen quite possibly was predisposed to Creationism as at this very time in history the orthodox had aligned themselves against Darwinism. In any event the Urantia Book covers this topic well, and the careful reader should conclude that neither polar position is accurate. G.J.C.

Life Beyond the Veil

knowledge that matter is indeed the result of vibrations, and that no particle of matter is still, but in ceaseless movement. That is correct, but not conclusive. For it does not pursue the matter to the end of it. It were truer to say, not that matter is in vibration, but that matter is vibration, the result of vibration of a quality more refined, which is found, not in the phenomenon of material things, but in those spheres proper to its quality.

Thus you will see how little it matters that, when the time comes for you to cast off the body of earth, you stand discarnate. Your earth body was a body of vibrations and no more. Very well, you now have a body of vibrations more substantial and enduring, because of a higher quality, and nearer to the energizing Will which brought it into existence, and so sustains it. That body will serve you while you sojourn in the lower spheres and, when you have progressed, that body will be transmuted into one still more permanent, and of quality more sublime. This process will be repeated as the ages go by and you proceed from glory to higher glory in the infinite reaches of progress before you.

It follows also that, as those in the lower spheres in this spiritual realm are not normally visible in the earth sphere, so those of the higher spheres are not normally visible in those lower spheres, and so on in like order as we rise from sphere to sphere and pursue our way along this glorious road of light and high endeavour.

So it is then, friend and ward, and when you come here one day you will be the better able to understand. For although you do now employ this same method, of which I have spoken in your own daily life, and so does every man, yet you little understand the manner of its working. Did you so it were well that all men be of one mind with us who try to use our powers for the glory and worship of God; for the weapon, to be used for good or evil, which man would then find to his hand would exceed in might and strength all his present knowledge; as that exceeds the mental endowment of the fly or little ant.

It is well that we are able to co-ordinate the progress in knowledge and in holiness that they journey together. For this is so—not perfectly, but within certain boundary lines, wide but sure. If it were otherwise the world would not be what it is to-day; nor order rule comparatively.

This, however, is one aspect of our care for the human

race; and what the future holds I cannot say. For I cannot see so far as to conjecture how far men will go in this new knowledge, the threshold of which they now have crossed. But things will be well ordered by those who watch with jealous care, and wisdom very great; and all will be well while this is so. †

Wednesday, December 3, 1913.

It may be well to pursue our subject in hand a little further in order that my meaning may be made more explicit. Know then, my friend and ward, that what I have said already in respect of the transmutation of energy is by way of defining, rather than explaining in detail, the use of my terms.

Consider the Heavens.

If you will look out into the display around you of God's life manifest in the elements of your sphere you will observe several points of interest.

First you would not be able to use the sense of sight to help you to understand His working were it not that light, which is external to you, were poured upon your planet. But light also is merely vibration, and also is not consistent in its vibrating quality from first to last. For you observe the sun to be visible, and the source of those vibrations. But outside the atmospheric envelope of the solar sphere those vibrations are changed in form by the variant medium into which they have entered. Thus the stream of light passes through regions of darkness, and so continues until it approach another atmospheric zone, such as that which is about the earth, when once again that energy is transmuted as to its quality, and becomes once again what men call light. Yet one entity alone is that stream from sun to earth, a stream of light energizing from its source, passing through a vast region of darkness, and emerging once again in its native quality wherever it strikes upon a planet in its course.

You will remember the words, "The light shineth in the darkness, and the darkness does not comprehend it." This, then, is more than an analogy merely. It is the mode of working which God adopts in His universe both of matter and spirit. And He is One;

and His Kingdom is one.

It is obvious, therefore, that certain conditions are necessary in order that light may become operative to reveal things to men. Those conditions are the environment upon which light acts, and by which it is also affected by reflex action.

So is it in respect of the spiritual environment. It is only when a genial environment is found that we spiritual ministers are able to become operative. And that is why to some we are able to reveal things in measure greater, and with greater ease, than to others whose environment is not so congenial. Whatsoever makes manifest is light, whether the thing manifest be material or spiritual.

And I tell you of another similarity. This is that as over the intervening region of darkness the light is directed from the sun to the planet far away, so from higher spheres is the light sent over the spheres intervening, and is received in the earth plane as direct, in a manner, as the earth itself receives the sun's light.

Now, look on another field. Far away beyond the farthest star you see from earth is a zone of wondrous beauty where suns have evolved to a much more conclusive system than those you observe. It is seen here that light is measured in proportion as heat is decreased; which would point to the fact that heat is by evolution of ages transmuted into those vibrations which constitute light. The moon is colder than the earth and reflects a greater light in proportion to its bulk. The older a system becomes the colder it grows, and more brilliant nevertheless. This is as we believe in my sphere; and I may tell you that no observed fact has to this present time been found to oppose our conclusion.

The Web of Light.

I once observed a very beautiful instance of the transmutation of energy here in my own land.

There was a company of visitors from another sphere, and they were about to return to their own, their mission having been finished. A party of our own, of whom I was one, went with them to the large lake over which they had come to us. Here they embarked in boats, and were giving us their parting words of thanks and goodwill, when one of our Princes was seen approaching with a company of attendants, from behind us. They came through the air and hovered about us and the boats while we, knowing their habits, but not their present intention, waited to see what manner of thing they—or rather, he, had in his mind to do. For it is a delight in these realms to give pleasure, each to other, by exercising such powers as we possess, and that in varying combinations by which effects are differently produced.

Far up in the heavens we saw them, as they moved slowly, circling about the Prince from whom to those in circle went threads of vibrations of different quality, and so of different colour. These he of his will sent forth, and those his subordinates wove them into a network of curious design and very beautiful; and where two threads crossed there the intensified light shone like a stone of brilliant hue. And the knots were of many colours owing to the varying combination of threads entering into their construction.

When this was complete the circle widened out and drew away and left their Prince alone in the midst. And he held the net by its middle in his hand, and it floated out around him like a many-coloured spider web. It was very beautiful.

Now, that net was really a system of many qualities of vibrations woven together. He released it from his hand and it began slowly to sink as he rose through it, until it was level with his feet. Then he raised his hands and descended with it. And as he came he looked through the net at the boats below; and he made slow movements with his hands in their direction.

Then they began to move on the water as of themselves, and so continued until they floated in a circle. Then the net descended and settled over them, and we saw that they were all within its circumference, and also that, as it lighted on them, they passed through it and it sank and rested upon the water. Then the Prince, standing on the net and on the water, in the midst of the boats, waved his hand in greeting to them. And the net slowly arose from the water, lifting the boats with it, and floated upward into the air.

So away over the lake they went together, and the company of our sphere closed in around them, and sent up a song of Godspeed as they floated away towards the horizon over the lake.

It was merely one of those little tokens of love which we here delight to show our brethren of other spheres of labour—nothing more. My reason for relating this—which was, in display, much more beautiful than I am able to show you thus in writing—was to illustrate the effect of the will of a powerful Angel Lord concentrated on the forces to hand and transmuting them in quality.

Beauty is not alone the minister of pleasure to the sight. It is rather a characteristic of these realms. For beauty and utility go together here. And the more useful a man becomes the more beautiful is he in person, the beauty of holiness is literal and real, friend; and it were well if all men could accept that truth. †

Thursday, December 4, 1913.

Having now explained, somewhat briefly, some of those principles, which are found in operation in your own sphere of earth, as also of these of more rarefied substance, I will continue in slightly different vein. For although it is not of your ability, nor helpful, to speak of those things which exist in these higher spheres alone more properly, yet a man must look ahead as he journeys; and the more he is able to understand of that land for which he is set out upon the road, the more sure will be his stepping onward, and less strange will appear that land on his arrival.

Beginning, then, at this point, it is one of the first tasks we have to learn here—having passed through the veil of flesh into the clearer realms of spiritual life, and having first to make familiar to ourselves the conditions found here, and that accomplished—to hand on to those who come on after us that same knowledge.

Spiritual Reality.

One matter which causes much distress and distrust to many souls is the fact that all they see here is real. You have already been shown this; but so strange it is and contrary to all rational expectation, that I would gladly add to what you already have received a little more. For it is of primary import to every one that he realize that the existence before him is no dream, as a man would say—but not we—but that it is indeed the fuller life developed, and the life for which the earth life is both a preparation and beginning. Why do men imagine that the sapling is of larger strength than the full-grown oak, or that the spring is of more reality and power than the river? The sapling and the spring are of your present earth life; the oak and the river are here.

The body you now wear, and the trees and rivers and other of material substance, which you call real, are not so enduring, nor so real, as their counterparts in these spheres. For here is found the energy which comes to your systems, and is as the electric dynamo to the single lamp as to its power and intensity.

When, therefore, men think of us as whiffs of smoke, and of our environment as drifting shadows, let them pause and ask if there is any sound reason to support their view. Nay, there is no reason in it whatsoever, but, on the contrary part, it is foolishness, and unworthy of thinking beings of spirit estate.

The Reality of Heaven.

Let me describe to you a scene in one of these spheres, or regions, as I will say to make it more natural seeming to you, a scene and an incident, by way of showing you what kind and manner of life you will take your part in one day soon. For when you step over into the sunlight, and think back to your earth life, it will surely stand out very vivid and plain, and the reason of things you now discern but in part will be seen to be both ordered and wisely beneficent. Nevertheless, how short a day will your present life then seem to you when around you unfolds ever one infinitude after another, and eternity begins to be of your life, which now you reckon day by day.

Far away a light is rising in the sky which overlaps the horizon like a violet-tinted veil, and seems to drop behind it, curtaining the further distance from my sight. Between that horizon and the high rock on which I stand to view is a wide-stretching plain. Here at my feet, far down below, I see a temple which, in its turn, is still high above the City which stretches round the base of the mountain.

Domes and halls and mansions surrounded by lawns of emerald, and flowers flashing and sparkling like gems of many colours I see, and squares and statues and fountains and many people, whose robes outshine the flower-beds and out-number their colours, move about in groups. One colour is seen to be dominant over the rest, however, and that is gold, for that colour is the principal of this City.

The City by the Lake.

High walls stretch, crescent-wise, along the outer part and embrace the City as the horns bend in towards the mountain on either side. On these walls are watchers,—not against foe, but to give tidings of what is forward out on the vast plain from time to time, and to welcome friends who journey here from regions far away.

The walls are lapped by the waters of a lake which is in extent as a sea or an ocean on earth would be measured. But yet it is possible for those who are trained to watch to see, beyond it, the land on the farther shore where the light is growing, and is seen kissing the sails and flashing oars of the ships as they go, some in one direction and some in another, upon the bosom of the gently swelling sea.

And now I descend and stand on the walls to watch what is enacting. Presently I hear a rumbling as of thunder coming from the direction of that violet cloud of light. This grows in volume and rhythm, and gains in pleasurable tone, until it has become one sustained chord of music.

Then from the temple above me I see emerge a great throng who wear white glistening robes, with golden bands about their middles, and each a fillet[22] of gold upon his head. These take hands upon the platform of rock before the Temple and, looking upward, seem to be lost in adoration. They are really gathering power to answer the salutation of the party who are travelling towards us beyond the horizon yonder.

Then another man comes forth and stands before them, looking towards the violet cloud of light. He is of larger build than the rest, clothed like them of white and gold, but more beautiful and bright of face, and whose eyes are like a flame of quivering light.

Presently, as they stand thus, a cloud begins to gather

---

[22] A fillet or circlet is a round band worn around the head and over the hair. Elaborate and costly versions of these eventually evolved into crowns, but fillets could be made from woven bands of fabric, leather, beads or metal. Fillets are unisex, and are especially prevalent in archaic to renaissance dress. Source: Wikipedia

around them and, as it thickens, we see it in movement revolving, until it takes the shape of a sphere, and is in colour golden, but full of many-coloured lights. It enlarges until at length it hides the Temple from view. And then a very notable thing ensues.

The sphere, revolving and sending out flash after flash of light—gold, crimson, purple, blue, green and other, slowly rises into the air, and higher still it goes until it is level with the topmost peak of the mountain behind and above the Temple. Higher still it rises, and its light radiates far afield. And I notice that the platform where stood the party of Temple-dwellers is bare of them. They have ascended in that globe of living light and flame. This is not possible but for those who have developed in training to endure that intensity of spiritual power which generates such phenomena as this. Higher still rises the sphere until it rests suspended, and the brilliancy of its flashing is increased.

Then I notice a shadow stealing from out its midst, and settling and spreading over that half of it which is opposite to the region behind; but the front which is toward the violet light in the horizon is naked, and its brightness is increased by so much that I may not look at it, but only at the rays as they travel high over the plain in answer to that message coming from afar.

Then, too, we hear a humming noise, like that of bees, which comes from the sphere of light; and this increases like the other, like a chord of great orchestras, as it swells out, high in the heavens now, and floods the plain and the sea both with light and music,—for here these are often made to go hand in hand, blended in condition and effect.

Our friends are seen and heard by those who come towards us from far away, and the two streams of light gradually approach, and so do the two strains of harmony, and all blend together in wonderful beauty. But they are not near together. That which in these realms answers to distance in yours is immense. These two in opposition are as if one of the stars you see from earth should salute a sister star billions of billions of miles away, and send her music to her in greeting, receiving answer in like responsive light and sound together blended. Then, could these two stars leave their moorings in the ends of space, and begin to come nearer each to other along the heavenly road, century after century, approaching at awe-inspiring speed and, for greeting sending out from time to time floods of radiance and music, as

Life Beyond the Veil

throwing kisses by the way, ahead of their meeting—so imagine this approachment of those two spheres of the spiritual universe, and you do not over-estimate either their beauties or powers of movement thus displayed.

I leave them thus, and go about my business, and all the time the light increases, and the people of the City tell the news, and hazard who it is who comes this time, and remind one another of who he meets, who came last, and what it was transpired then of glories new and not before seen in that city while they had been citizens.

So each goes about his work in happy expectation, for all visitors here bring joy, and joy receive in themselves of their hosts, and take it back to their own people when they again depart.

Now, I would that I might describe for you the meeting. That I am unable, for it is of those things that are not possible to utter in words of earth. Even thus far I have been much hampered, and have only found it possible to picture the scene previously by lopping and chopping off all the more beautiful parts and giving you just a skeleton frame to hang your imagination upon. If the glory of it all in separation be tenfold more glorious than I have been able to write, what shall serve me of language to tell you of the blending of those two glories when they were come together? The heaven was transformed into a blaze of light, and thousands of beings flashing here and there, with many species of transport animals, and wagons of different construction, and banners and devices, and flashing, radiating, shimmering lights and colours, and voices which were like instruments of music falling upon us below, as they wheeled and circled in the heavens above, like showers of golden rain mingled with violet flowers and diamonds.

Rhapsody? Yes, friend, to those who would measure heaven by earth's drab pageants, tawdry and tinsel in their trappings, and enacted in an atmosphere which to this of our own land is as fog to sunlight. Yet in the midst of all the dull dampness of earth and earth life, you yourselves are not of earth but of those heavenly Spheres potentially and by reason of your destiny. Be you, therefore, not so sordid to grovel about with nose to earth smelling for gold which decomposes itself, and is not of lasting and persisting quality. Use what things you have, and be glad that your world is so wisely ordered and so wonderful as it is, but do not rate this land by what you find normal in that lower sphere.

Highlands of Heaven

Look onward, friend and ward, for this is yours; and all those beauties and delights we hold in trust for you. Stretch forth your hand in faith, and I drop into it just one small gem of all these heavenly treasures. Open your heart to us and we will breathe into your being some of the music and love of your own future home.

And so, be you content awhile, and do what you find at hand to do. We keep your inheritance sure and safe for your coming, and, so you do your work as faithfully and as well as you are able, you and all such shall come to us as Kings and Princes of the Blood—of the Blood—which is His Life for all who love holiness as He loved it and, because He loved its beauty, did not flinch to do His Father's Will—at Whom men scoffed, and for which they crucified Him.

Tread in His way, for that way led Him to the Throne, and shall lead you there, you and all who do their parts nobly and with love.

Of such He is their King. †

Monday, December 8, 1913.

And now, my friend and ward, I am of a mind to-night to continue that of which I made a beginning when last I impressed you.

That violet cloud of glory and the one of my own sphere were commingled and, as I looked up at the sight, I saw, as I told you, the movement of those who were within. Then the glory settled down upon our City, and all the buildings and trees and people and all things therein were bathed in that violet-golden shower, and took on a more lovely aspect by reason of the baptism.

For you will understand that it was from a sphere more advanced than my own from which these our visitors were come; and none come so but they bring a blessing in gift to leave behind. Thus when they had departed we had received that which enabled us nearer to our next step onward, and the whole city glowed with somewhat more of sublimity than heretofore.

Now, it chanced that I had business in the Temple at that time, and there I made my way along the mountain path. It was a long ascent, but usually I went afoot by way of meditation and preparing of myself for whatever I had in hand on such occasions as this.

Old Comrades Meet.

Here and there along the path ascending are shrines, set a little off the way, like those in many lands of earth. And as I stood before one of these, a little removed, I covered my eyes with my hands, and stood thus awhile to commune with Him Who of His Life gives strength to us to follow after Him in the Heavenly road. Thus it was that I did not hear when some drew nigh me until their steps were present with me on the path behind. Then they ceased and I, having finished my offering, turned and saw those whose light showed me of their degree that it was not as mine, but higher in the spheres. So I bowed myself to them, and stood with eyes to look upon the ground, and waited for them to tell of their will and purpose with me.

But I stood for long and they did not speak to me. So, making bold from the silence of them, I raised my eyes and looked upon them, first at the girdle of their robes to understand of what order they might be. Thus I understood that they were of those messengers who attended their Chief on his journeyings. Such they were as you shall call them aides-de-camp to their Leader.

Then, they still continuing in silence, I looked on their faces. They were aglow with smiling; and amusement was not lacking in their smile. So I steadfastly gazed upon them, and at first I could discern little, for it was no easy matter that I should penetrate through that radiance shimmering around them then, to see their features whether I knew them or no. But, catching some of their power, as is the manner at such times, I did at length come to a knowledge of their countenances. Then I understood. They were two old comrades who, when we did service nearer to the earth plane, had fought for souls and won them out of the darker regions into the light of the Presence. And I had been their minister then, and their companion.

They came to me, when they saw the dawning recognition in my eyes, and, taking each a hand in his, we went together up the hill, and on towards the Temple plateau, they kissing me first on either cheek, and so imparting to me further of their strength, to be and to converse with them.

Oh, the bliss and the great pleasure of that walk, when

they who had been advanced beyond my present estate spoke first of old times and service together and, gradually leading, came to present times in this my own sphere, and then spoke, in sequence, of their own more bright and glorious, to which soon, perhaps, I should be called.

The Temple and its Sanctuary.

So we came to the Temple, and the way seemed not so long by much as at other times for the beauty of their presence and the entrancement of the talk they gave me of the added glory of their Home.

They bore a message to the Temple-keeper that their Chief and Lord would sometime soon come, with our own Ruler, to bless the Temple and to offer worship there, both for his own retinue and himself, and for the City at which, for the time being, he was guest.

Will you describe the Temple to me, Zabdiel?

What I am able in your words at my disposal I will give you.

There is no wall between the facade and the edge of the precipice, so that the Temple is seen most clearly from the plain a little out from the City walls. It rises sheer from the platform of rock, one arch topping another, and mounting upward in perfect harmony, and in colour growing lighter as the higher arches are reached. The dominating colour I cannot tell you, for you have no such on earth. If I name it a combination of pink and grey that is all I can do; and it does not give you a very exact idea of its aspect. But let that suffice, and indeed I come little nearer in my description of the architecture itself.

There is not one great porch (verandah) alone, as in most of your cathedrals, but there are five. They are of different build and hue, and are so constructed for the accommodation of those who come here to worship. For were all to be admitted through one gate, those of lesser power would experience an enervation which would take from their ability to worship when within. So these five door-ways are made to lead them into that nave where they may recover to be strengthened. Here they pay their first vows and devotions. Then they pass on into the great central hall of the Sanctuary, where they all mingle together without discomfort.

Life Beyond the Veil

There is a square tower over this central space, open to the top and to the sky above. And over the tower hangs a moving, luminous cloud, which is like the Shekinah of old, the Dwelling Place from which, at certain times, descends into the Temple, and upon the worshippers, an access of His Life and blessing.

On the farther side of this space there is another nave; and here are angels who come to meet with those who are called. These minister to us by teaching of those Mysteries which are of the Higher Realms, and only those who have progressed much may receive their teaching, for it is both very high in wisdom of Divine things and powers, and also it is given sparingly, for, as a moth is destroyed of the flame it seeks too eagerly, so it is not with impunity that the higher Wisdom may be either had or given.

Into that inner Sanctuary I never yet have looked, for my time is not yet at hand to do so. And when it comes I shall be ready. I shall not be bidden there before I am fully prepared. Yet before I am advanced to my next sphere onward I must pass through the learning to be had there, and there alone. Towards this I am at present endeavouring.

I have told you somewhat of that mighty Shrine, but falteringly, for it is too glorious to put into your words. Of such a theme St. John of the Revelation strove to tell to those his brethren who had been less favoured than he. But he could but tell them of precious stones and pearls and light and crystal and no more. Well, that is my present case, my brother, and I am at pause. So let me leave it there with some sorrow that I can do no more than this which falls so short of the glory which crowns and suffuses all that Temple which stands on that Heavenly Mountain in the Tenth Sphere of these long reaches of progress in knowledge and wisdom and power and strength and blessing towards Him Who is the Source and Spring of them all. †

Zabdiel, I feel it rather a strain to come on succeeding days. Would you rather that I came on every other day; or on every day I can, as at present?

As you will, friend. Only remember this: that the power is here now, and it may not continue. I will sustain you for so long as I am able, and when that fails by reason of your limitations—then I can no more. I will make my journal so completed as I can, however, while you are in this state of receptivity. But do as you think well. If you decide to continue daily, then do not overload

Highlands of Heaven

your mind with other writing more than is necessary for your dutiful fulfilment of your obligation to your people and friends. Take exercise and recuperation out of doors, as you feel it helpful. And I will give you what I can of my strength and sustenance. But my ability to give is greater than is yours to receive. So, if you feel able, come daily, or as nearly so as your duties permit. We have not once failed previously on any day, and may be able so to continue.

Chapter 6

The Summerland of God

"Teach me Thy way"—The glade of the statue—Flora of the Tenth Sphere—The Sanctuary of Festivals—A Heavenly vista—The meeting at the Valley of the Peaks—The meeting with Harolen—To the Gate of the Sea—Laus Deo—The altar on the raft—"One Lord, One Faith"—A Heavenly Transfiguration—The Son of Man.

Tuesday, December 9, 1913.

So you come to me, my ward, as I desired you. I think you will find my endeavours none too feeble but that I shall be able to say some little thing which will be of help to you, and to others, to-night. For there are forces on hand which will enable you when you do not know it, and I use them to put my thoughts in order before you. So do not hesitate in your distrust of your own faculty to reproduce them. When you are no longer fortified to do so I will inform you, and we will close up our book for the time being and give our minds to other matters.

Now give me your mind that I may continue on my way, for I would like that to-night you should be given to know a little further of our doings here in this Tenth Sphere. Only remember always that I am constrained, and that of necessity, in my narration, to model my description, in some measure, on the conditions as they are found in the spheres lower than this of mine, even as, once again, these pictures are further reduced within the compass of the language and imagery of earth. This of necessity, I say, for it is not possible to put a bushel of wheat into a pint measure, nor to confine light within the darkness of a leaden casket.

"Teach me Thy Way."

The Temple-shrine of which I spoke is of use not for worship alone, but for instruction of those competent to receive it. This is the High School of the sphere, and only those who have passed through the lower forms may come here for their final learning. At various points in that region are other schools or colleges, each for some special class of instruction in wisdom, and some few for the co-ordination of some of these branches together.

The City itself has three of these colleges, where those who have passed through what I will call the provincial schools come to learn the relative value of the various teachings they have received, and to combine them together. In many spheres this line is followed. But each sphere is both continuous, and also in advance of, the sphere inferior to itself. So that from the lower to the higher spheres there is a graded system of progress, and every step onward implies an added capacity, not alone of power, but in enjoyment in the using of it.

Instructors are mostly of those who have qualified for the next sphere in advance, but who elect to stay in order to teach those who, in their turn, shall succeed them when at length they go on into their own proper place of abode. From time to time these instructors do make their journey into the sphere above, and then return to continue their task. For they are enabled to bear its enhanced glory, while those who are of lesser degree are not able to do so.

And also there come once and again those of the higher spheres into the lower for friendly intercourse and conversation with their fellows who teach there; and then they nearly always are willing to condition themselves according to the environment of that same lower sphere, in order that they may impart some loving words of encouragement to the pupils.

When a spirit from one of these spheres descends to your earth, it is necessary, in order that he may make contact with you who dwell there, to condition himself in like manner, and this in more or less degree. So it is here between the higher and lower conditions obtaining in the spheres of various quality and elevation.

But it is easier for us to commune with some of you than with others, and that according to your degree of advancement spiritually. So again, is it here in the spirit land. There are those in the Third Sphere who know of the presence of those of the Fourth or Fifth or even higher spheres, by reason of their advancement spiritually beyond their fellows. If to these latter such visitors wish to become visible and audible they must the more completely condition themselves to the environment of that sphere, and this they do.

This description is in outline, and you will see that what seems at first to complicate life here really serves to its orderly arrangement. The leading principles which govern the communion of saints on earth with those passed higher are produced here, and continued on into the higher places upward in orderly sequence. And if you wish to know what regulates our own communion with those above us, then reason it out by analogy, and you will have as fair a knowledge of it as is possible to you while still on earth incarnate.

Thank you. Would you describe a little more in detail the City and the country of the Tenth Sphere?

Yes. But first as to the name "Tenth Sphere."

That is what we name it by way of brevity. But in every sphere other spheres are found to touch it. What we will call the Tenth[23] is the dominant note: but the harmony of the spheres is one and blended. For this reason a man may aspire to that above him, and is lifted up by reason of the contact of that higher zone interpenetrating his own.

But also, having progressed to, let us say, the Seventh, he is initiated into all those spheres below, through which he has passed. Thus, just as others come down to him, so too he can go down to others, so he conditions himself always according to that sphere into which he goes. And he may from his own sphere reach forth his power to those in the spheres below. This we continually do, even from our own projecting our awareness, and power to aid, into the earth for those with whom we have established contact. We do not always leave our own home when we help you;

---

[23] As has already been mentioned, the sphere naming scheme in use in this series is different to that used in the Padgett Messages and the Urantia Book. The difference is simple, the numbers have been doubled here and thus what is termed the Tenth Sphere here is the Fifth in the other two sources. Obviously this finer graduation serves the purpose here because it provides a definition of what would be sub-planes within the spheres in the other two sources, and as long as one knows how to convert from one to the other, there is no confusion. G.J.C.

Highlands of Heaven

but on occasion we do so, as necessity compels.

Where are you now—in your own, or here in the earth sphere?

I am now calling to you from nearby. For, although I count little of bricks and mortar, yet, on account of your incarnate condition, and your inability to rise far towards us, means I must meet you on the way. So I come to you and stand within call of you, or you would produce my thoughts, but not in the order and manner I wish. And now to answer your inquiry of this land which is my own. Bear in mind the words with which I began to-night, and I will tell you.

The Glade of the Statue.

The City stretches round the base of the mountain. Between the walls of it and the Lake are mansions and their grounds which extend left and right, and most of them approach the Lake itself. We embark on the water and take a straight course ahead and, landing on the opposite shore, we find it is wooded with trees, many of a kind only found in this Sphere. Here also we find paths set out and, taking the one before us, we go a long journey inland, and at length emerge into a glade.

In this clearing there is a statue. It is that of a woman who stands looking upward into the heavens above. Her arms hang down against her sides, and her dress is a plain robe without ornament. The statue was placed there long ago, and has stood gazing upward for many ages.

But you are spent, my brother, to-night. So I must leave this theme and renew it, if I may, at another time. Look up, as the face of that statue does, and you shall receive a baptism of light upon your eyes that you may see some of the glories which are there. †

Thursday, December 11, 1913.

To continue: The glade in which the statue stands is one where we often meet to receive direction from those above us who, from time to time, find it convenient to call us away from the throng of our brethren in order that they may commend to us some line of special study to be done. Here we meet and they come to us and in that beautiful glade are more beautiful than the setting in which they shine.

Flora of the Tenth Sphere.

Out of the open space lead several paths. We take one to the right of the further side, and pursue it. On either hand as we go we see flowers blooming, some of the daisy family, and the pansy, and others standing aloft as if rejoicing in their beauty of foliage and colouring, like the dahlia and the peony and the rose, All these, and more too; for we in this sphere know no flowers in their seasons, but all bloom together in the perpetual, but never-wearying summertime.

Then, here and there are other kinds, and some are of great diameter, a veritable galaxy of beauty, like great shields of flashing light, and hues all beautiful, and all giving forth delight to the beholder. The flora of this sphere is beyond description to you, for, as I have already explained, there are colours here which earth knows not, by reason of its grosser vibrations, and also because the senses of the human body are not enough refined for their perception.

Thus, to digress a little, there are colours and sounds about you which are not recognisable by your senses. And here we have these, and more added, to help the gorgeous display of loveliness, and to show us some little of what the Beauty of Holiness must be like nearer to the Central Bliss where the Holiest dwell in the Heart of the One Alone.

The Sanctuary of Festivals.

Presently we come to a river which bisects our path, and here we turn to the left, for we must visit a colony which will be of interest to you. And what, think you, do we find here at the edge of the forest which bends away from the river and leaves an open plain to view? Naught else but a Sanctuary of Seasons or—shall I say?—Festivals.

Now, you in the earth plane have only a small sense of the nearness of us who seem to you so far away. Why, not a sparrow falls but your Heavenly Father knows and marks it. So all you do is open to us, and scanned with interest and much care, if perchance

Highlands of Heaven

we may be able to throw into your worship, from time to time, some sprinkling of heavenly dew which shall tincture it and you with thoughts of Heaven.

Here, then, in this colony are curious[24] ministers who seek to weigh your Festivals on earth as they come round year by year; and these add their own offering to that of those who attend your worship[25] to strengthen them in their helping of you as to that particular bent of mind which directs your thoughts and aspiration at the greater Festivals of your cycle.

This is not of my own special work, so that I do not speak expertly. But I know that all those ideas which with you do cluster about such as Christmas and Epiphany and Easter and Whit Sunday and the like are reinforced from such colonies as these.

I have heard, moreover, and believe it true, that those who worship the Father God by other rules than the Christian are likewise tended at their great Festivals by their own special guiding, watching angels.

Thus it is that you will note at such times an added fervour in the worshippers at their Shrines of grace, and much of it, I believe, is the result of streams of spiritual power directed from these schools, and flowing into the hearts of the congregations on earth, united in praise and worshipping of God.

You would like something to be told of the buildings of the settlement. There are many, and most of them are lofty. And they assemble around a dominant structure which rises on many arches and is storied far and high into the space above. The top of this is spread out and hangs, with lip-like festoons, over the houses below it, as it were a lily opening ever but never quite fully in bloom. It is of blue and green, but shaded in its folds with rich brown, like gold intensified. It is lovely to look up to, and speaks of worship unfolding heavenward, like a flower whose perfume ascends while the very heart is expanding itself to the gaze of those above, and to the Heavenly Creator and Lover, Who is over all, and yet sees and knows and finds pleasure in the breathing of the heart's life back to Him Who gave it and sustains it unceasingly and forever.

We leave this beauteous flower to hover like a bird with

---

[24] Meaning "zealously careful" (old use).
[25] In other words, spirit attendants.

mother-wings above her brood of clustering dwellings which fondle one another below and seem safe in the protection, as it were, of their mother Sanctuary and Shrine. We leave these and continue.

After a long journey up-river we begin to ascend, and continue. Thus we come to the Mountainland; and here we look far away into the distance. This is on the borderland between our Sphere and the one next in ascent. Some of us are able to see farther and in more detail than those who have not developed themselves as much. What I see I tell you now.

A Heavenly Vista.

We are on the summit of a mountain, which is one of many. Before us is but a little valley and then rises range after range of higher peaks and summits; and the farther you move to focus your gaze the brighter is the light which bathes them. But that light is in no way still. It moves and shimmers and dazzles and darts among those far mountains as if they lay within an ocean of heaving crystal or of electricity. That is the aspect, and I can do no more than that for you.

Streams and buildings there are, but these are far away. I know that among those mountains there is grass, and there are flowering plants and trees and meadows and gardens and mansions of those who dwell in that Sphere. But these are not visible to me, who can only see the outstanding landmarks.

And over all, and throughout all, I see the Love of God and His most exceeding and excellent comeliness and beauty: and my heart leaps forward to rejoice with me on my way. For there I am going, and, when I have fulfilled my task here as it is given me to do, and not until then, I know that some fair denizen of that enchanting land will come and call me, and I shall leap in joy to hasten there.

Ah but, my brother, is it not thus with you also? What that farther sphere is to my own heart, the next of your advancement should be to you, and as lovely by comparison.

I have told you but only a very little of this sphere, but enough to give you zest and appetite to urge forward on your march.

I would now come back to the glade and bid you keep your

eyes full steady gazing upward. Nay, your foot shall in no way stumble because your eyes are not groundward bent. For those who look aloft look in the way they are going; and we look downward to keep your stepping sure.

So all is well, my ward; yea, all is well for such an one, for, because he trusts us who serve our Lord, on Him his heart is firm; and none shall make him stumble.

So be it, then. The world is dull and wearying, times and oft, yet there is beauty, too, and love and holy aspiration. Take of these and enjoy them. Give of them freely to others, and the gloom will seem less gloomy, and the light beyond will dawn more clearly and brightly, and the sons of the morning will lead you on into their own more lovely Summerland. †

Friday, December 12, 1913.

The Meeting at the Valley of the Peaks.

Standing on that high peak radiant with the light which strikes it from the realms behind me, and bathed in the greater light of those before, I commune with those of both spheres and, through them, with the spheres beyond. Such moments are of bliss too great for utterance, and open the eyes of spiritual understanding to see things glorious and mighty, and infinitudes vast, and all-embracing love.

Once I stood thus, with face turned towards my future home, and closed my eyes, for the intensity of light as it moved before me was more than I could bear continuously. It was there I first was permitted to see and speak to my guide and guardian.

He stood upon the summit over against me opposite; and the valley was between. When I opened my eyes I saw him there, as if he had suddenly taken on a visible form for me, that I might see him the more plainly. And so it was indeed, and he smiled on me, and stood there watching me in my perplexity.

He was clad with a glittering silk—like tunic to the knees, and round his middle was a belt of silver. His arms and legs below were bare of covering, and seemed to glow and give forth the light of his holiness and purity of heart; and his face was the brightest of all. He wore a cap of blue upon his hair which was like silver just

Life Beyond the Veil

turning into gold; and in the cap shone the jewel of his order. I had not seen one of this kind before. It was a brown stone and emitted a brown light, very beautiful and glowing with the life which was all about us.

At last, "Come over to me," he said; and I was thereupon afraid, but not with any terror, but rather abashed of awe. In that way I feared, not else.

So I said, "I know you for my guide, sir, for my heart tells me this much. And I delight to look upon you thus; for it is very lovely and sweet to me. In presence you have been with me often on my heavenly road, but always just before, that I have not been able to overtake you. And now that I am given to see you thus in visible form I am glad to thank you for all your love and tending. But, my lord and guardian, I fear to come to you. For, while I descend into the valley, the brightness of your sphere will dazzle me and make my feet unsure. And when I should ascend to you I think I should faint by reason of the greater glory which is about you. Even here I, from this distance, feel it scarce to be borne for long."

"Yes, for this time," he replied, "I will be your strength, as many times before I have been, not always of your knowledge; and at times again when you have known me near but only in part. We have been so much together that I am able now to give you more than previously. Only be strong, and with all your courage to the fore; for no harm shall fall upon you. It is to this same end that I have impressed you to come to this place, as often I have come to you."

Then I saw him for awhile stand very still indeed, as if he might well have been a statue. But presently his form took on another aspect. He seemed to be in tension as to the muscles of his arms and legs; and I could see, beneath the thin gossamer—like garment, that his body there was in like manner exerting its every power. His hands were hanging at his side, and turned outward a little, and his eyes were closed. Then a strange thing happened.

From beneath his feet there came a cloud of blue and pink mingled; and it moved across from him to me until it was a bridge between the two summits, and spanned the valley below. It was in height little more than that of a man, and in breadth a little broader. This gradually came upon me and enveloped me, and when I looked I could see him through the mist, and he seemed

Highlands of Heaven

very near.

Then he said, "Now come to me, my friend. Tread firmly forward to me, and you shall have no hurt."

So I began to walk to him through that shaft of luminous cloud which was all about me, and, although as I went it was elastic beneath my feet, like very thick velvet, yet I did not sink through the floor of it into the valley, but continued my way uplifted with great joy. For he looked on me and smiled as I went to him.

But although he seemed so near, yet I did not reach him, and yet again, he stood still and did not retreat from me.

But at last he held out his hand and, in a few steps more, I had it in mine, and he drew me on to firmer footing.

Then the shaft of light faded and I found I stood on the further side of the valley, and looked across to my own sphere. For I had crossed over by that bridge of heavenly light and power.

Then we sat down and communed together of many things. He called to my mind past endeavours, and showed me where I might have done my task in better ways; and sometimes he commended me, and sometimes did not commend, but never blamed, but only advised and instructed with love and kindliness. And then he told me something of the sphere on the borderland of which I then was; and of some of its glories; and how the better to sense his presence, as I went about my task to which I should presently return to finish it.

And so he talked, and I felt in very good fettle of strength and delight, and of greater courage for the way. So did he give me of his larger strength, and of his higher holiness, and I understood a little more than previously of man's potential greatness, in humility, to serve his Master the Christ, and God through Him.

He came back with me by way of the valley, with his arm about my shoulder to help me with his power; and we talked all the way down and across, and then, as the ascent of the hill on the other side began, we slowly fell to silence. Instead of words we communed in thought and, when a little way up returning I looked upon him, I noticed that I could not see him quite so plainly; and began to be sad at that. But he smiled and said, "All is well, my brother. Always it is well between you and me. Remember that."

Still he grew more faint to my sight, and I was minded to turn back again for that reason. But he impelled me gently and, as

Life Beyond the Veil

we ascended, he surely faded away from my sight. I did not see him thus again. But I knew him now as I did not till that time. I felt him in touch with me all the time I lingered on that summit. I turned and looked into the brightness of his sphere across the valley, but I did not see him on the other side.

Just as I was turning to depart, however, I looked again, and I saw a form speeding over the mountain peaks beyond; not a solid form, as his had been, but one almost transparent. Like a ray of sunlight he went away from me visibly, or partly so; and that sight, too, slowly faded. But yet I felt him present with me, felt that he knew of me, and what I thought and did. And I turned to descend with much joy, and greater strength to do my work awhile.

If from that brighter sphere such a blessing is given to me, shall I not in turn hand on some little to those who need it as greatly as I do? And this we do, my charge, through those heavens below our own; and even to you on earth we come and minister with much gladness. For it is very sweet to do to others our brethren what so bountifully is done to us.

I cannot make a bridge for you, as he did for me; for the variance of degree between the earth sphere and this is, at present, too great to be treated so. But there is a way by which to cross at the appointed time, as He has said. And His power is greater by far than that of him who made the road for me across the Valley of the Peaks. Of Whom I am a very lowly servant. But what I lack in degree of holiness and wisdom I strive to supply in love, and if we do both serve Him as we are able, He will keep us in peace, being reliant on Him across the depths from glory to the greater glory which is beyond. †

Monday, December 15, 1913.

I left that spot uplifted for the work I had to do before that time when I should be called hence to be as he is. Oh, the beauty and high peace of that place, and of him who is my guide. If the people of that farther zone are but half so beautiful and so lovely as he, then indeed a blessed race is that to whom I am on my way.

But now, my brother, it is upon me to help you on your way. And this I would, but by little or by much, so I add something to enable you and others on the road I sometime trod myself. Reach me your hand, then, and I will, on my part, do what I am able.

I left that place, I say, uplifted, and from that time my own environment was the more plain to me, in that I had viewed it from on high afar to see the outstanding matters in their right proportion, and from time to time I do this now when some problem more vexed than others perplexes my understanding of it. I view it as from the high places nearer that farther sphere, and things resolve themselves more orderly-wise, and become more plain.

This do you, my ward, and life will then appear not quite so much in a tangle; but leading principles will take their place of right, and the Love of our Father be more plainly seen. In order thereto I will continue to describe for you more of this sphere in which my present work is cast.

Descending, I turn to the right hand from the river and, taking a road which bends around the wood some little distance away from it, and through a plain bordered on the right by mountains, I go my way alone in meditation.

The Meeting with Harolen.

Presently I meet a company of those who have their dwelling farther ahead, and these I will describe to you. They are some afoot, and some on horses, and some in wagons, or chariots,—open vehicles they are, of wood, and with gold about them for a binding and bordering, and also devices on their front parts which tell of what realm and order the riders are. The garments of the throng are of many colours, but the dominating one is mauve deepening into purple. There are some three hundred men of them, and I receive and give salutation and inquire where they are bound, and on what manner of business.

The one I speak to falls out of the line to answer me. He tells me that word has come to his city that a number of those of the Ninth Sphere are about to receive their initiation into this the Tenth, having qualified by their conduct. On hearing this I beg that he will speak to the leader that I may accompany them in order to see what is about to happen there, and also that I may add my welcome to their own. On this he smiles, and tells me to walk with him and he will vouch for my acceptance. "For," adds he, "he you call the leader walks side by side with you."

At this I turned and looked on him, greatly surprised; for he wore a purple tunic, truly, but it was without ornament, and the fillet on his head was also a purple band with but one red jewel in it, and no device. Others were much more richly clad, and to look upon more comely and princely. I did not say so much, but he was of development greater than I, as I had already began to suspect, and knew my thoughts without their utterance.[26]

So he smiled again and said, "These new-comers shall see me as I am at this time; for some among them, I am told, are hardly ripe for much display of radiance. So they shall be as glorious as I, and they will not be dazed. Have you not lately had an encounter, my brother, as will serve to show you that too much glory may possibly impede instead of help?"

I confessed this to be the truth, and then he said, "You see I am of that sphere to which your guide belongs, and stay here in order to finish my task as I myself elect to finish it. So I condition myself in such ways that those our brothers and sisters who come here shall feel the homeliness of home till they be ripe for the glory of the Court. So come, my brother, and we will overtake those yonder before they reach the river."

We did so and crossed the river with them, swimming it, men and horses and wagons, too, and came to the other side. We left my city on the right, and went on to the pass which goes between the mountains where the scenery is very large and massive. Rocks rear themselves with much stateliness on either hand, like spires and towers and domes, and they are of different colours. Here and there vegetation grows and now a plateau is seen stretching away between the shoulders of two hills, and on it rises the chief city of a colony of happy people, who come and look down on us from aloft, and wave their salutation, and throw flowers to us as love-tokens.

---

[26] There is a big difference between what one might call active thoughts, and past memories of thoughts. More advanced spirits can recall all past thoughts of those they meet who are below them in advancement, thus enabling them to understand perhaps even better than the spirit does, their position on any issue. But active thoughts are easily read by any present, as this is how conversation generally is conducted. G.J.C.

To the Gate of the Sea.

So we pass along and at length emerge into a valley which opens out on either hand, and very beautiful it is here. Groups of trees cluster about fair and stately mansions, and some, of the more homely kind, of timber and stone; and lakes there are and streams falling with sweet music into the river which runs onward from the mountains round which we have come into the distance before us. Here the valley closes again, and we see two giant pillars of natural rock through which the road must pass side by side with the river.

We emerge through this Gate, which the Valley people call the "Gate of the Sea," and before us we see the open ocean, into which the river falls from a great height, and is very lovely to see as it falls, like many thousands of kingfishers and humming-birds making their many-coloured flight down the mountainside, flashing and sparkling, into the waters below. We descend by pathways and stand on the shore; but some still remain behind to watch for those who shall come over the sea. We are well timed, for our leader has powers which are of the sphere beyond, and is able to use the forces of this zone with so much the greater ease. He has so arranged affairs that, but a few moments after we have taken up our station on the shore, a shout is raised by our watchers above that the company is in sight far out at sea. Then round the bend of shore beyond the river come a company of our ladies who, as I learned when I asked, had their homes in that district in order that they might join those who came to that shore from distant lands.

Great was the rejoicing of us all to greet them, and theirs to receive and give greeting in return.

Then high upon a rounded summit, below which their home was, we saw their Mother standing. She was robed from head to foot in silver gossamer, and shone through her robe like a beautiful glittering diamond or pearl endowed with life and fresh vitality. She looked intently at the party on the sea, and then began to make a weaving movement with her hands.

Presently we saw a large bouquet of flowers was taking shape between her hands. And then she changed her movements, and it began to float out and stretch itself into a rope of flowers which went out into the air, high up across the waters, and at length it rested over the people who were on the sea.

Then it drew itself inward, and began to form a flat spiral, and circled above their heads awhile, and then gently settled down upon them, and broke up into a shower of roses and lilies and other kinds of flowers, which fell upon them and about them. As I looked I saw their faces change from inquiring expectation into glad smiles of happiness, for they understood the token they had received, and knew that love and beauty awaited them in this new sphere to which they had journeyed far.

Now I was able to see the fashion of their ship. Indeed it was no ship at all, but a raft. How shall I speak of it simply? It was a raft, indeed, but it was no bare structure, for there were upon it couches and beds of soft down, and instruments of music; and of these the chief was an organ on which three men were now beginning to play at one time,—all these and other things of comfort. And at one side I noticed what looked like an altar of offering, but in detail I cannot speak of it, for I do not know the use of it explicitly.

Laus Deo.

Now the organ begins to sound, and the people afloat break forth into an anthem of praise to the All-Father, to Whom every knee bows in adoration, for from Him only is Life, and all are through Him enabled. The Sun shines forth His life to earth, and the Heavens are as chambers within the Sun for light and warmth of love. To Whom, and to all those Gods Who owe Him birth and due allegiance, be our duty paid in offering of a pure heart and will of loyalty.

Now, these words were of a strange tone to me. But when I heard them, and the music which bore them through the air, I looked once again at the Altar, for I thought to find in it an answer. But this I could not. There was no sign or emblem upon it by which I might interpret this thing. It was but later that I was able to come at the meaning of it.

But you grow towards the end of your powers for this night, my ward. Therefore we will cease now, and I will take up my theme again to-morrow, if you will. To-night God give you His blessing, as ever. So, good night. Zabdiel is with you in thought and communion through the day and the night. Remember this and you will understand whence come many thoughts and suggestions——No more now. You begin to tire. Zabdiel. †

Wednesday, December 17, 1913.

And so we now proceed on to the further account of the coming of those from the far land across the sea. For their voyage had been a long one by way of preparing them against their taking up residence in this their future home.

Now, they had disembarked upon the shore, and all were gathered beneath the high headland which stood above like some giant watch-tower. Then their leader looked among us for our Chief, and at last espied him, and knew him. For they had met before. So he came to him and the two greeted each one the other with warm love and blessing.

They conversed together for some time, and then our Chief stepped out and spoke to our new brethren, somewhat thus: "My friends and brethren, children with us of the One All-Father, Whom all adore according to that light he has, I bid you welcome to your new home.

"You have come far to seek it, and it will not disappoint you when you explore its beauties. I am but a humble servant here, but as it is to the Colony over which I am set that you will be led to begin your manner of life here, I am sent thus to welcome you.

The Altar on the Raft.

"As you well know, and have learned by a long course of training, the faith you once held was but one single ray of the whole sunshine of God's great Love and Blessing. In the course of your instruction and development you have come to understand so much as this and more. One item alone of your own peculiar manner of worship have you retained—the Altar I see upon your vessel. But inasmuch as the distinguishing device has faded from its pedestal, and as I saw no smoke of incense rise as you neared the shore, in offering of thanksgiving and adoration, I think that, as a token and badge, your Altar has lost some, or all, of its meaning to you. It is for you to choose whether you will bring that with you, or leave it aboard to return it to the land from whence you came for the use of others less progressed than yourselves; or whether you will land it, and convey it with you into your new life here. Will you, of your courtesy, consult together, and tell me?"

Then they held a conference, but not for long; and their spokesman said, "My lord, it is even as you say. There is now little meaning left to us in that which once was of aid to know and worship God our Father. For we have, by much teaching on the part of others, and our own meditation, come to know that all God's children are of one birth and race, as children of the One Father Alone. The time is now when it helps us no more to remember anything which divides, even though it be in love and general tolerance. We would, therefore, send it back; for yonder are those who perhaps remember more of the details of that religion which we have now progressed beyond.

"And now, my lord, we follow you to learn, of your goodness, and that of our brethren who serve under your guidance, what more we may of the Brotherhood of all mankind in the light of this brighter land, and those realms which lie beyond."

"You have very well said it," replied the Chief, "and it shall be so. Had you chosen else it would have pleased me; but this choice pleases me the better. And now, my brothers and sisters, come, and I will lead you into the fields which lie beyond this Gate, and into your Home."

So saying, he mingled with them, and kissed every one upon the brow; and I noticed that, when he did this, their countenances became of a more luminous aspect, like our own; and their clothing became more radiant also. And the Mother descended from her station aloft, and did as he had done. They were so happily met with us, and we with them, that we did not hurry to depart. Also their leader came some way with us for company; and we set off through the Gate, while the Mother and her maidens sang a hymn of Glory to the Highest, and to us a welcome and farewell in one. So we took our way inland along the valley.

Now, you will wonder at that Altar, and at the meaning of the speech of our Chief—

If I might interrupt you, Zabdiel, why do you avoid telling me his name?

I will tell you his name as you may put it into these letters, but cannot render it to you in its essential manner. Moreover, that is not permitted me. I will call him Harolen. That has three parts in speaking it, and so has his; and it will serve very well. So, to proceed.

He was much in occupation among the throng until we had passed the valley and river and were well into the country, the aspect of which I have not described to you previously, for it was beyond that spot where I first met him. Then, when I noticed he had leisure, I approached and asked him who these were, and what worship they and he had spoken of on the shore. Harolen answered, in effect, that they in the earth life had been worshippers of the God Whose Name was wrapt in the Fire and in the Sun, and Whom the old Persians reverenced.

"One Lord, One Faith."

Now, I must add to that, of my own knowledge, this, ensuing. You must know that, when people first come out of the earth life into the first stage of their life eternal on this side, they are as they left the earth. This much you know. They who have any serious religion at all continue their worship and manner of life and conduct according to that religion as to its main and leading principles. But as they progress there is a winnowing, and the chaff is blown away, one fistful after another, as they go on from sphere to sphere. Ye while some shoot ahead, the bulk linger and go more leisurely onward; and those who have left them behind come back to them, from time to time, to instruct them.

So they go on from age to age, and realm to realm, and sphere to sphere; and all the while they approach nearer to the Universal idea of the All-Father. Brethren they still are together; but they learn to welcome, and then to love, brethren of other modes of religious thought and belief; as these others do also. And so there is a constant and increasing intercourse between those of varying creed.

But it is long before most will merge together in absolute unity. These old Persians still retained many of their own peculiar ways of looking at things, and will do so long hence. Nor is it to be wished for otherwise. For everyone has a character of his own, and so adds of his own to the commonwealth of all.

But that party had made one more step onward during that

Life Beyond the Veil

voyage on the sea. Nay, rather I would say that during that voyage they had been brought to realize that they had already progressed that one stage in advance. Thus it came to pass that while certain of their phrases, and the way they made their adoration, gave it, to my mind, a distinctive tone and turn, yet that was more of the outer than the inner. And when the test was given them they decided to leave that Altar behind them, and to go onward themselves into the wider Brotherhood of God's Household of the Heavens.

It is thus we leave to float away into the mists behind us one after another of those minor helps which on earth seem so wonderfully important. It is thus we learn here what Love and Brotherhood really mean.

You are troubled, my charge; for I can both see and feel your mind and self at variance. Let it not be so, my brother. For know and be well assured of this: whatsoever is real and good and true will endure. Only what is not as these will fade away. And He Whom you serve is indeed the Truth, but did not reveal to you all truth; which was not possible to be done for those who are subject to the limitations of the life as you live it incarnate on earth. But He said you should be led into all the truth; and that is seen proceeding in the spheres beyond the bounds of earth. Of such I have even now been telling; and this leading continues I know not into what eternities of existence, or into what infinites of expansion in wisdom and love and power sublime.

But this I know—I who, as you, did worship and homage to the Christ of God and of Nazareth, and who pay my reverent devotion now as you are not yet able—this, I say, I know, my ward and fellow-worker in the Kingdom, that He is still much further on. The light that would blind me is to Him in His holiness as the twilight is to me. Beautiful He is, I know, for I have seen Him as I am able, but not in His fullness of glory and majesty. Beautiful He is, aye, and lovely as I cannot find words to tell. And Him I serve and reverence with glad devotion and great joy.

So do you not fear for your own loyalty. You will not take from Him by giving reverence to our brethren of other faiths than ours. For they are all His sheep, if they be not of this fold. Who is, and was, the Son of Man, and so Brother of us all. Amen.†

Thursday, December 18, 1913.

Highlands of Heaven

The territory through which we passed was hilly but not mountainous, and on every side were green knolls, and here and there a dwelling. As we went Harolen became slowly changed in aspect. He grew brighter of countenance, and his robes began to assume a more luminous appearance. By the time we had progressed past the woodland on our left hand he was come into his normal beauty and appeared thus. On his head a symbol of light appeared, as it might be a crown of jewels of red and brown, which sparkled and shone forth their rays, and between the rays and about there hovered an emerald radiance. His tunic fell to his knees, leaving bare his arms; and a gold belt he wore about his middle, clasped with a jewel of pearl-like substance, but in colour green and blue. His cap was of like colour, two-tinted, and on his forearms were zones of gold and silver interwoven.

He stood in the wagon, which had two wheels and was very beautiful in wood and metal, and drawn by two horses, white and brown. I noted that brown seemed to be in evidence throughout, but not so much as to give distinction to that colour but, as it might be said, to underlie every device, in a way that its presence was seen, and yet its aspect was subdued.

Symbolism in this land is of much interest and greatly used. I, therefore, seemed to read in this scheme of his colours the fact that he belonged to an order and realm in which brown was distinctive but, serving in this lower sphere, while present out of appropriateness, yet those other colours which are more familiar among us in this sphere were given a place about him who had elected to serve here some time longer than of necessity he might have done.

But as I looked on him, thus so simply garbed and yet so altogether beautiful, I felt his great power. For in his eyes there shone clear holiness, with dignity to command, while his brow, over which his brown hair parted and curled backward about his temples, seemed to woo humility and gentleness as a sister more beloved. Yet he was such as no one of lesser estate might willingly dare in opposition, while none would fear him, so that one be simple in his good intent and loving nevertheless. One he was whom to follow his lead was joy, and in whose protection and guidance implicit trust might well be placed. For he was a Prince, with a prince's power, and wisdom to use it aright in gentleness and love.

A Heavenly Transfiguration.

So we journeyed on, not much conversing together, but drinking in all the beauty of that place with much gladness of heart, and peace and rest about us. Thus we came at last to the place where the new-comers should pause to stay awhile until they had become familiar with their new environment. Then they would proceed farther inland to one of the settlements, and perhaps would go some to one and some to another, according as they were the better fitted for this or that in the work and service of this sphere of the Kingdom of God.

Arriving here Harolen called a halt, and asked for silence for a little space, as he had a message to bring to them from his chief city, which lay ahead beyond the rising hills and out of sight.

So we kept silence and, presently, a great flash of light shot through the heavens from some point beyond the hills in front. It struck upon us and we stood all bathed in a flood of brightness; but no one was startled or afraid, for the light had joy in it. But if it clothed us, then about the chariot in which the Prince stood was a very glorious thing to be seen.

He stood there quite still, but the light about him became focussed and concentrated; and he appeared no longer as he had been previously, but, as it were, transparent and all aflame with glory. How shall I give you some small idea of what I wish to tell? Try to picture him made of alabaster, but living and glowing and irradiated through with a beauty of glorious light, itself alive and rejoicing. Every jewel and ornament became suffused with it, and the chariot itself was glowing as with flames of fire. And all about him were glory and the majesty of life and energy. The horses, also, did not so much absorb as reflect the radiance. And the circlet about his head shone forth with a sevenfold intensity.

Yet he did not rise into the heavens, as well he might have done, so translucent and sublimated had he become in appearance. He stood there still, his eyes looking straight into the light and reading it as a message, as if he saw what we could not see, and that, too, not there but far away ahead over the hills, at the place from which that light was sent.

The next we knew surprised us all greatly. Instead of

compelling some wonder or miracle of power, he quietly knelt down in his wagon, and bowed his face into his hands, silent and still. And yet we all felt that he was not afraid, but master of that light, and of even higher majesty. We knew he bowed to One of greater might and in holiness higher than he. So we, too, knelt and bowed to worship Whom he worshipped, knowing a Power was present, but in whose Person we did not know.

The Son of Man.

As he knelt thus we presently heard music and voices chanting some very beautiful theme, but in words we none of us could interpret. Still kneeling we looked up and saw that Harolen had descended from his wagon, and stood upon the road in front of us, his company. Walking down the road towards him was a Man, clad in white from head to foot. One circle of light crossed His forehead and girded His hair behind. No jewel did He wear, but over His shoulders two bands, which were crossed between His breasts before, and were held in place with a belt. They and it were of silver and red mingled. His face was calm, and with no majesty save that of love and kindness; and He walked with slow and thoughtful step, as if He bore in His heart the weal and woe of some great universe. It was no sadness we saw, but something near akin, and yet I cannot name it, so unfathomable was that quiet all-embracing calm which was about Him.

He came to where Harolen still knelt, and said some word to him in a tongue we did not know; and also His voice was so subdued that we felt He spoke rather than heard Him. The Prince looked up then into His face and smiled; and his smile was lovely, as everything about him was lovely. Then the Other bent down and folded him in His arms, and raised him up, and stood by his side and held his hand in one of His own. Standing thus He raised His right hand and, looking on us, He blessed us and spoke words of cheer and encouragement to proceed in our work which lay ahead of us.

He was not eloquent, but rather were His words those of a mother to her children setting forth on a journey. No more than this, and spoken so quietly and so simply, and yet in a way that gave us confidence and joy together, and all fear was taken away. For at the first we were somewhat in awe of Him before Whom our

Prince had bent the knee.

    Standing thus, the light all gathered itself together and enveloped Him, and while He held the hand of Harolen He became more and more invisible, and then was gone from sight where He had stood. And the light was gone, as if He had absorbed it into Himself, and had taken it with Him when He went.

    Once again our Prince knelt down upon the road, and bowed himself awhile. And then he arose and in silence, waving his hand to beckon us onward. He mounted his wagon in silence, and in silence we followed him round a hill till we came to the place nearby where these should stay. †

Chapter 7

The Highlands of Heaven

> Zabdiel's Tour of Inspection—At the Children's Home—A lesson in creative faith—At the village of Bepel—Joy and sorrow of the Angels—Into the Highlands—The Highland Watch Tower—How messages are received there—An Horizon of Glory—Walls of light—Motherhood enthroned—The Crimson Glory of the Christ—A colony with a problem.

Friday, December 19, 1913.

"ACCORDING to your faith be it unto you." This stands a promise of power to-day as when first He said it; and it may be claimed with full assurance of fulfilment. Only that faith must be present, and then the present enablement will be manifest, in ways diverse but with no uncertainty of cause and effect.

Now, this is not alone to you, but to us here in these spheres progressed and progressive. It is the acquiring of faith in exercise that we study to compass and, that gotten, we are powerful to help others, and ourselves to enjoy. For it is delight and pleasure to give, more than to receive, as He said.

But do not mistake the nature of faith in the using of it. In the earth life it is of indefinite quality as mostly understood—something between trustfulness and a right understanding of what is truth. But here, where we study all things as to their essence, we know that faith is more than this. It is power capable of scientific analysis, in a measure in correspondence with the progress made by any man.

In order to show you my meaning the better I will tell you of one incident in which this is seen.

At the Children's Home.

I was making a visit to certain homes at the request of my Superior, to see how they did who lived in them, and to help by

Highlands of Heaven

what advice I might, and to report on returning. So I went from one home to another, and came at length to a cottage in a woodland part, where there dwelt a number of children with their guardians. These latter were a man and his wife who had progressed, in the latter period of their ascending, side by side. These had the care of the children, boys and girls, who had been either stillborn, or who had died at birth or soon after. Such are not, as a rule, taken to those Homes in the lower spheres, but brought higher for their development. This is because there is little of earth to remove out of their natures; and they also need more special care than those who have, even by a little, fought and developed in the earth battle of life.[27]

The guardians greeted me, and the children came, at their beck, to pay me their welcome. But they were very shy, and did not easily respond to my talk to them at first. All these children are very delicate in their beauty who come over here so, and I was very loving to them, these little lambs of our Father and His Son. So I encouraged them, and at length they became more relaxed.

One little man drew near me and began to play with my belt, for its brightness pleased him, and he was curious about its metal. So I sat on a little grass bank, and took him on my knee, and asked him if he would choose what pretty thing the belt should bring him. He was doubtful of what I meant at first and, following that, of my ability.

But I repeated my invitation, and he replied, "A dove, please you, Sir." That was very polite of him, and I told him so, and that when little boys asked in such ways, trusting and believing, then they always got their will, if that will was wise and pleasing to our Father.

A Lesson in Creative Faith.

This saying, I placed him on his feet before me, and put out my will to the end he desired. And presently the form of a dove was seen in the plate of metal which fastened the belt, and this

---

[27] This issue was only clarified very recently and relates to the issue revealed in the Bible (Exodus 34:6-7) where it is said the sins of the parents and grandparents are passed to their children. The channelled message is located on the new-birth.net web site. G.J.C.

Life Beyond the Veil

grew in distinctness, until at length it expanded beyond the plate, and then I took it, and it was a live dove which stood on my hand and cooed, and looked at me, and then at the boy, as if wondering which was the parent of its being. I gave him to the lad, and he took him into his bosom, and ran to show the others what had come to pass.

Now, this was no more than a bait to hook more fish. Surely they came, by one and two, until a little crowd of eager faces looked up into mine, not daring so much as to ask, yet longing to be brave enough to do so. Still I waited and said nought, but only smiled them back their smiles; for I was giving them a lesson in the power of faith, and their acquirement of it demanded some initiative on their part.

It was a little maiden who was first brave enough to express the wishes of herself and her companions. She stepped forward and took the border of my tunic in her little dimpled hand and, looking up to me, said rather tremulously, "If you please, sir—," and then broke off and coloured with confusion. So I hoisted her to my shoulder and told her to ask her will.

She wanted a lamb.

I told her that orders were coming in in some good style, and growing in bulk betimes. A lamb was rather a bigger pet than a dove. Did she believe that I could give her a lamb?

Her reply was very naive. She said, "If you please, sir, the others do."

I laughed heartily, and called them nearer, and they said, Yes, if I could make a dove with feathers, I could make a lamb with wool on it (but they called it fur).

Then I sat down again and spoke to them. I asked them if they loved our Father, and they said, Yes, very much, for He it was Who made all this beautiful land, and showed people how to love them. I told them that those who loved the Father were His true children, and that if they asked Him for anything wise and good, believing He was present in His life and power, they would be able so to make their wills use that power that the thing desired would come to them. So it was not needful that I should make any more animals for them, as they could make them themselves. But, as this was rather a difficult case to begin with, I would help them.

Then, at my bidding, they all thought of the lamb they wished to, have, and then willed that it should come to them. But

Highlands of Heaven

nothing came of it apparently; and I restrained my power on purpose. After trying awhile I told them to pause.

Then I explained that they were not powerful enough yet, but when they grew bigger they would be able to do even this, if they continued to develop their faith, in prayer and love, and continued, "For you have that power, only it is not yet large enough, except to do small things. And I am going to show you that you have some of that power in you now, so that you will continue to learn your lessons from your good guardians. You have not yet sufficient power to create a living animal, but you have enough to influence one already alive to come to you. Are there any lambs on this estate?"

They said there were none, but there were some on an estate rather a long distance away, where they had gone on a visit a short time before.

"And you," I said, "by your faith and power have brought one of these lambs to you."

I pointed behind them and, turning, they saw a little lamb feeding on a path among the trees a little distance away.

They were too much surprised at first to do anything but stare at him. But some of the older ones recovering broke away and ran, with cries of delight, to the place where he was and, seeing them, he ran sporting and prancing to meet them, seeming as joyous as they to find playmates to sport with.

"It's alive," they cried, and turned to beckon the laggards on; and soon that poor lamb was smothered with fondling and caressing, as he might have been a child of their own begetting. I do think they exhibited a considerable sense of motherhood and ownership.

Now, this may seem more or less casual, according to the perspective of him who reads. But it is essentials which matter. And I tell you that the pretty little lesson thus given was the spring of what will eventuate, perhaps long ages hence, in the creation of some cosmos, as it might be that of which your planet is a small member. It is thus the Principalities and Powers began to train for mightier things. What they had seen me do was an act of Creation. What they had themselves done, with some little aid from me, was the beginning of such evolution which should lead them on to do what I had done, and then to progress, as we in these spheres do, from power to power greater still as faith is added to, little by

Life Beyond the Veil

little, as we use it in the service of Him Who gives it to us to enjoy.

This is faith, and, unseen by you, or not so clearly seen, your faith it is which, sanctified by prayer and high motive, brings to pass its own fulfilment. Use it, then, but with care and circumspection and all reverence, for it is one of the great trusts which He has confided to you—and to us in greater measure—and that is no mean mark of His great love. Whose Name be blessed for the free Bounty of His giving. Amen forever. †

Monday, December 22, 1913.

At the Village of Bepel.

Thus far, then, of the children's home and schooling. And now to other matters of that tour.

I entered a village where some small number of houses were grouped, but each in its own small domain. Here were there several miniature communities of people who had in hand occupations dissimilar in detail only, but in general on the same line of development. The head man of the place came to meet me at a bridge which spanned the stream which wellnigh circled this village and passed onward, eventually emptying its waters into that river of which already I have spoken. Our greetings made, we passed on together. As I went I noticed the neatness of the gardens and dwellings, and remarked on it to my companion.

Could you tell me his name, please?

You may write it down, Bepel. Let us continue.

I came to one, however, which was not so attractive, and on this I also remarked, and asked the reason why; for I was not acquainted with what reason it might be which, in this sphere, should arrest the progress of any.

Bepel smiled and replied, "You know the man who lives here, he and his sister. They came over from the Spheres Eight and Nine some good while ago together. Here they progressed and, from time to time have returned to the Fourth Sphere, where they have loved ones and, in especial, their parents. This they have done in order to help them onward. Lately they have come to be some little less at their ease in these surroundings for the love they bear to those behind. It would seem that these are making their progress very slowly, and it will be long before they reach this estate. These two, therefore, await the coming of someone who has authority to permit them depart to take up their abode with those they wish to help, in order that their more continual presence should be at the disposal of them to enable them onward."

"I will see these two," I replied, and we went within the garden.

Now, you may be interested to know how such a case as this is dealt with here, and so I will proceed, in more or less detail, to describe what followed.

I found the brother in a small coppice to the side of the house and accosted him, inquiring for his sister. She was within, and we went to seek her. We found her there in deep meditation. She was engaged in communion with her parents far away in that other sphere. Rather would I say that she was sending her help and uplifting strength to them, for "communion" implies a mutual action, and the others were little able, if any, to return their thoughts to her.

So I talked with them awhile, and gave them my conclusion after this fashion: "It would seem that the strength required to build up your own progress in this Sphere is being drawn upon by those in the Sphere some degrees behind. You are held back by the love of those who are yonder, and slow to progress. Now, if you go to that Fourth Sphere, and there take up your habitation, you will be able to help them a little, but not much. For when you are at hand why should they stretch forth to come beyond their own present degree? It is not well, therefore, that you go to them in such manner as that. Yet love is greater than all else, and as it is found both in you and them, it will be of great might to prevail when obstacles which now obstruct have been removed. I would advise that you do not relinquish your degree of this Sphere, but that you come with me to our Chief, and I will ask that he will give you other work to do by which your own progress will be ensured, and that of your loved ones not hindered."

When I departed they came along with me and, after consultation with our Chief Lord, I was glad to find that he, in the main, approved of what was in my mind. So he called them, and gave them words of support for their great love, and told them that, if they would, they should become of those whose mission it was from time to time to go to the Spheres behind and, there appearing (by conditioning themselves to the environment of the sphere in which they should be), deliver what business he should have to communicate. On such occasions he would request that their parents should be permitted to see and talk with them. By so doing they would be lured onward and upward to join these their two children in those higher realms.

He further counselled great patience, for that this thing might in no way be forced ahead, but must progress by natural development. To this they assented with much joy and gratitude of heart. So the Chief Lord blessed them in the Name of the Master, and they departed to their new home well content.

So you will see from this, my friend and ward, that in the higher realms of progress problems arise which feature those of the spheres just ahead of the earth plane. For many there too, are held back by their love of those on earth who do not progress so that they may come into communion with their spiritual lovers and helpers, and therefore do not ascend many degrees above the state of these incarnate laggards.

But others there are, also incarnate, who, by their own advance, do but by a little, or not at all, hold back their spirit guides, advancing after them by strenuous endeavour, with humility of heart and holy aspiration, that they help the rather, often, and hinder not at all.

Keep this also in your mind with the many other things you have learned. It is possible, nay, inevitable, that you who are incarnate on earth do help on or pull back your good friends on this side.

Joy and Sorrow of the Angels.

In which light think of the Angels of those Seven Churches to whom the Christ sent word by the hand of John. For those each, by the virtues or sinfulness of the Church he had in charge, was judged in person, as through that Church accountable to Him Who assessed each in its exact value, and awarded praise or blame to the Angel-guardian of each Church according as it merited the one or the other. As the Christ, the Son of Man, identified in Himself the character of the children of men, and held Himself accountable for the salvation of His brethren according to the flesh before the Father, so is each Angel-guide accountable for, and identified with, the one, or the community, over which he is placed to serve. He enjoys with them, and suffers with them; he rejoices over them, and mourns over their shortcomings. Remember what He said, for this I have seen, not once, nor two nor three times, but many, "There is joy of Angels before the Presence of God in the Heavens when a sinner repents." And I add to you, my brother, the bright Angels do not always laugh—though laugh they do, and that in constant. But Angels, too, can weep tears—weep and suffer for your sorrows and sins who fight the fight below.

This will not be in tune with the thoughts of us in many minds. Never mind, write it down. For by what reasoning do we joy, if we may not also mourn? †

Tuesday, December 23, 1913

For all that it is so plainly written that men and angels work together in the one service of God, yet men find it hard to believe this to be true. It is because they give too much thought to the things of earth, and too little to the origin of material things. This is not of those forces which come immediately into contact with matter to shape and use it, but beyond, where they use those forces as a potter uses clay to make his jar or vase. This has, in some degree, already been given to you to write down. Tonight I will tell you some narrative of their doings as we see them at their work from this side the borderline.

Not all are progressed evenly in any one of the spheres, but some are advanced beyond others. Those of whom I last told you were of the least in this Tenth Sphere. I will now tell you of some who have risen to greater life and power.

Into the Highlands.

On my way, as I journeyed after leaving the village where the brother and sister dwelt, I paid my visit of inspection to many other settlements. One of these lay among the mountains towards the zone which marks the beginning of the next Sphere superior to this—not that spot where I met my guide, but at a similar altitude, and some distance away. Here I ascended by a winding path which led to the high lands among the summits of the mountain range. When I began to ascend the grass was very green and the flowers large and profuse. Birds sang about the velvet path among the leafy trees of forests deep with purple lights and shadows, and many spirits of the woodlands worked with bright smiles as I passed them, giving and receiving, greetings of blessings, and adding joy to beauty by the way.

Then the surroundings began to change, and the trees became more stately and statuesque, the forest less dense and leafy. Whereas before glades of flowers and arbours of foliage had been, there now appeared lofty cathedrals of pillars and arches, as the trees stood up and bent their heads to make them. Deep and lovely still were the lights and shades, but more like those of a sanctuary than of a bower. Of large proportions were the avenues, as I passed them, stretching away on either hand. Here, too, there was a sense of meditation and greater power than away below. And I was aware of spirits in the colonnades who were beautiful with a grander and holier beauty than those I had left behind about the first rises of the hills. This also, as I went, gave place to scenes more amazing and inspiring. Gradually the tree country was left behind, and about the white, gold and red of the summits played lights which told of presences from the higher realm descended on some business, to linger among these heights awhile.

So I came to my destination. I will describe it as I am able. There was a flat space, perhaps a mile in square each way, paved with alabaster stone, which appeared of flame colour, as if it were a floor of glass stretched over a realm of fire whose rays played about it, and glowed through, tinting the air for some hundred yards above. There was no fire of such sort. But this is how it appeared.

The Highland Watch-Tower.

On this level space was one building. It was of ten sides, and each side was diverse in colour and in architecture from all its fellows. Many stories it had, and rose a glittering pillar whose top caught the light which came above the peaks of the mountains, some far, some near—so high was this tower, as it stood there, a sentinel among the mountains of heaven, a very beautiful thing to see. It covered some eighth part of the square, and it had porches (verandah) on each side. So there were ten ways to enter, and one facing each of ten ways. A sentinel in truth it was; for this is the Watch-tower of the highest regions of that sphere. But it was more than this.

Each side was in touch with one of the first ten spheres; and those who watched there were in constant communication with the Chief Lords of those spheres. There is much business passing between these Heads of the different spheres continually. Here it was gathered up and co-ordinated. If I might descend to earth for a name, I would call it the Central Exchange of that vast region comprised in all those spheres stretching from that which borders on the earth zone, over the continents and oceans and mountains and plains of the second, and then of the third, and so onward to the Tenth.

Needful it is that those who serve here be of very high development and wisdom, and so I found them to be. They were different from the ordinary inhabitant of this sphere. They were always courteous with love and kindness, gentle, and anxious to help and gladden their brethren. But there was a stateliness of absolute calm upon them which never gave place to the slightest agitation whatever news came to them there of the doings and strenuous life they held in direct contact with themselves. They received all reports, information, requests for solution of some perplexity, or for help in other ways, in perfect quietude of mind. When something more tremendous than usual burst upon them, they were unmoved and ready always, quietly confident in strength to cope with their task whatever it might be, and with wisdom to make no mistake.

I sat within the porchway of the side which was in communion with the Sixth Sphere studying some of their records of past events and their concern with them. As I read, a quiet voice whispered over my shoulder, "If you are not too much interested, Zabdiel, in that book, you would perhaps enjoy to see what we do within." I looked round and up at him who spoke, and met his quiet beautiful smile with a nod of assent.

How Messages are Received There.

I went within. There was a large hall of triangular shape and, high up, the floor of the next apartment. We went to the wall, where it met in angle, and there my friend bade me stand awhile and listen. I soon heard voices, and could discern the words they brought. These were being dealt with in a room above us, five stories aloft, and were transmitted downwards, passing through the floor into the ground below, where there were other chambers. I asked the reason for this and he informed me that all messages are received by those who had their station on the roof of the building. These extracted what words they needed for their part of the work, and allowed the residue to proceed downwards into the chamber below them. Here the message was treated in like manner, and again handed on downwards. This was repeated again and again until what was left passed down the walls of this ground-floor room to be once again sifted and the residue passed on below. In each room there was a great multitude of workers, all busy, but without haste, going about their task.

Now, you will think this a strange way to go to work. But the reality was stranger still. For when I say I heard the words, I only tell you half. They were audible visibly. Now, how shall I put that into your tongue? I can no better than this: As you gazed at the wall (which was treated in different metals and stones, each vitalized by what principle here answers to electricity with you) you saw the message in your brain rather than optically and, when you were sensible of its import, you heard the voice which uttered it in some region far away. In this manner you were aware, in your inner consciousness, of the tone of the speaker's voice, of his aspect and stature and manner of countenance, of his degree and department of service, and other details of help to the exact understanding of the meaning of the message sent.

This dispatch and receipt of messages is brought to high perfection in these spirit realms, and in this Tower of Vigilance to the highest perfection I have encountered. I was not competent to translate what I saw and heard, for the communication had come through the conditions of all those spheres intervening, and had become more complex than I could unravel. So he explained it to me simply.

It was to the effect that a party had been sent from the Sixth Sphere into the Third to, help in the construction of some works there proceeding. Those who had designed them had been of high development, and had included in the apparatus and structure to contain it, a somewhat more advanced scheme than it was possible to construct successfully out of the substance of that sphere. I might put the problem to you thus: If you were to endeavour to build up a machine for the manufacture of ether, and the conversion of it into matter, you would find no substance to your hand on earth of sufficient sublimity to hold the ether, which is of a force greater and more intense than any force which is imprisoned within what you understand as matter.

It was a somewhat similar problem they had to encounter now, and wanted advice as to how best to proceed in order that the scheme might be carried out to as large an extent as possible. This is one of the simpler problems these high ones are given to solve.

Now, I will tell you more of this at another time. You are spent now and I cannot find words in you to say what I would.

My blessing is upon your life and work. Be assured thereof and go forward bravely. †

Christmas Eve, 1913.

I have spoken of the science of that High Place and it would not be much of help to you were I to continue in that vein; for the wisdom and duties there are of a degree you would understand but little. It would confuse you, and seem not over-wise, what I could give to you. I will, therefore, briefly add what I may, and get on to another theme.

I went up to the storey next above, and found it and the rest full of business, with workers at it in plenty. The walls of these large halls are all utilized in the sifting of messages and other like work. They are not flat walls, such as you know, but all shimmering with vari-coloured radiance, and embossed with devices, and otherwise relieved. All these are instruments of their science, and all are watched, and their effects recorded and considered and handed on to their proper destination, whether to others within that settlement, or to spheres higher or lower, as the business in hand demands.

An Horizon of Glory.

My kind guide took me to the roof of the Tower, and here I was enabled to view the country far afield. Below me I saw the woodlands by which I had ascended. Further away stretched range on range of high mountains, all bathed in the high celestial light, and glittering like jewels of many colours. About some of those peaks there played a shimmering beauty which reached them from the Eleventh Sphere; and they seemed to be alive and responsive to the presence of high beings whose nature was of a degree so refined that their forms were just beyond the circumference of visibility to one, like myself, of the Tenth Sphere.

Yet I knew that these were come over from their own brighter region, and were on some work of love engaged in this my own. At that I rejoiced very much for the knowledge of the love and power beneficent all about me, and my only speech was silence, which spoke more eloquent than words of mine could do.

At last, when I had thoroughly feasted my spirit on this great beauty, my companion gently laid his hand on my shoulder, and said, "Now these, my good brother, are the HIGHLANDS of this HEAVEN. The solitude is such as, in its beauty, fills you with reverence, awe and holy aspiration. For you now stand at the summit and boundary of your present attainment; and you have here found an environment into which, of your own strength, you are not able to penetrate. But it is given to us, as a sacred trust, and to be used sparingly and with discretion, to unveil the veiled, and look on that which is invisible to our normal sight. Would you that this, for a few moments, be given to you, that you look into what is around you unseen till this present?"

At this I paused, somewhat afraid, for what I saw was as much as I had strength to endure. But, while considering the matter, I resolved that where all was love and wisdom, no harm should be able to strike me. So I entrusted myself into his keeping; and he said it was well.

Then he turned from me and went into, a Sanctuary which was upon the roof of this Tower, and was absent awhile, as I told myself, in prayer. Presently he came forth, and he was changed greatly; for his robe was not upon him, but he stood naked before me but for a circlet of flashing gems upon his brow. How beautiful he was as he stood there bathed in that soft penetrating light which intensified about him and moved and lived, until his body was like liquid glass and gold and shone forth increasingly till I looked downwards and shaded my eyes from his exceeding brightness.

Walls of Light.

Then he spoke to me and told me to stand before him, while he would keep to my rearward, using his power upon me, but not blinding me with his radiance. Thus we stood, his hands upon my shoulders, and the light from him enveloping me also, and, streaming forth on either side of me, it shone far out blending into the distance with those other lights far away about the peaks. Thus a lane appeared in front of me where I stood, its either side bordered with a wall of light, and the space between not dim but of lesser brightness.

I could not penetrate those walls with my vision, as they swept away across the deeps and heights of the mountain-tops, opening out as they went, on either side in such wise that, while I stood, as it might be, in the angle where the two walls of living flame met just behind me, yet in front it was a space of great breadth between the walls where I could see them far away.

Then he spoke again and told me to watch this space. I did so, and there grew a vision very wonderful upon my gaze, so that I who have beheld many beauties and marvels have never seen anything so entrancing as this.

The two rays struck one on either side of a mountain peak which rose into the sky, a sharp needle with lesser spurs about it below. As I looked it began to change, and I saw a large Temple emerge into my view, and about it were a host of high angels in robes of light, moving here and there. There was a high porch (verandah) and upon it stood a great Angel who held a cross aloft, as if he showed that symbol to some congregation of people in some other far-away sphere. On each arm of the cross stood a child, one in rose-pink garments, the other in green and brown. They sang some song I could not understand, and then, as they ended, each laid his hands upon his breast and bowed his head in worship.

Motherhood Enthroned.

But my guide now turned me about to the right and another vista came into my range of vision. Upon a hillside far away I saw a Throne. It was of light and fire mingled, and there sat upon it a woman who looked in silence into the far, far distance unmoving. She was clad in gossamer which sparkled like silver as her body shone through it; but over her head was a robe of violet-coloured light which fell upon her shoulders and behind her, framing her beauty such that I thought of a pearl hung against a velvet curtain.

About her, but below her Throne, were her attendants, both men and women. They stood there before the Throne and on either side, silent and waiting. They were all of much more brightness than I, but none was so radiant as she who sat there serene in all her loveliness. I noted her face. It was full of that carefulness which is born of love and pity, but her eyes were dark in their depth of high wisdom and power. She rested her two arms upon the arms of the Throne, and I noted further that all her limbs told of strength, but such strength as is mingled with the gentleness of motherhood.

Then suddenly she stirred, pointed with her hand here, beckoned there, and waved to others, as she issued, in no haste, but briskly and incisively, her commands.

All suddenly the crowd was in movement. I saw one party rise and fly off like a flash of lightning into the distance. Another went in other direction. And other groups I saw bring forth horses, mount and ride away into space. Some wore flowing robes, and some were girt with what looked like plated armour. Some parties were of men, others of women, and others of men and women both. In, as it were, a moment's time, the sky was dotted with diamonds and rubies and emeralds, as these appeared flashing on their heavenly way; and the dominating colour of the group shone back to me, as I stood to gaze in awe and silence.

Thus the lane of light was moved from place to place the whole horizon round and, at each pause, something new to me I saw. Each scene was diverse in character, but of equal beauty with the rest. In such manner I saw some of those who were of higher degree than any I had yet beheld at work in the service of the Father. And when I saw, by the changing light, that my friend had withdrawn once more into the Sanctuary behind me, I sighed for bliss too great, and sank down overcome with the glory of the service of God as I had seen it in operation among those who watched us as we, too, worked, and took account of our needs.

It was thus I came to understand, as never before, how that all the inferior spheres are included within those above, and not lying sharply defined, away each from its fellows. This Tenth Sphere included in itself all those below and was, in its turn, included in those above, together with the others below the Tenth. This is well understood here, up to our own degree. But as we advance, this inclusion of spheres becomes more complex and wonderful, and there are things to understand in it which are unfolded but by little and little. This I have come to see, and am all agape for the further advance when I am ripe for it.[28]

Oh, the wonder and beauty and wisdom of our God!

If what I know be but a little of His scheme of love, then what must the whole be like, and how tremendous!

Veiled are even the lower glories of the Heavenly Lands from mortal eyes, which strain to see them. Brother, be content to go slowly in these things. Such things are veiled in love and mercy. For, could they burst upon you in their fullness, your mind would give way before it all, and you would for long, long ages fear to go ahead lest worse befall you. I see it now as once I could not. It is wise and good—all wise and altogether good. And He is Love indeed. †

Saturday, December 27, 1913

The Crimson Glory of the Christ

Now, it was very wonderful that I should thus be permitted to see these wonders of those spheres beyond my estate. I thought about it afterwards, and found I could understand some of the principal intention and motive of what I had seen; but there were many things else I could in no way fathom unaided. One was in this manner of appearance.

The whole heaven between the two ends of the light-rays, which formed each a wall on either hand of my prospect, was flooded crimson. Deep, deep and intensely deep was the region,

---

[28] This design of the Spirit Spheres is remarkably similar to a diagram found in a later book authored by Robert James Lees called "The Gate of Heaven." I would reproduce it here, but it requires some explanation, so I will leave that to those interested enough to read the book, which is in the recommended reading list. Note this also uses the sphere numbering of 1 to 7 rather than 1 to 14 found in this series. G.J.C.

Life Beyond the Veil

on which I gazed, with crimson light. It seemed to be some gigantic volcanic upheaval, for clouds of this luminescence heaved and swayed one upon another, and lifted up great hunks of itself on high, and swept to the one hand or to the other hand, and sank and met other banks of cloud. All was commotion as of blazing and consuming catastrophic fury. So awe-inspiring did that red maelstrom seem to my soul that I trembled very much in fear of it.

"Turn me away from it. Of your love, sir, turn aside to some scene less awe-inspiring. For this is of mystery too terrifying for me to uphold myself before its overbearing grandeur."

Thus I besought my friend, who replied, "Rest you awhile, my brother, and you shall see it is not terrifying any more. You are now looking towards the higher spheres, the first of these being Sphere Eleven. In what sphere that light shines I cannot tell you, unless I afterwards read the record of it, and this is not taken in this College, but in one some distance from here.[29] For this you behold is far beyond our duties to deal with. It may be Sphere Thirteen, or even Fifteen, upon which you now look so much afraid. I know not. But this I know—the Christ passes there, and the Crimson Glory you see is the aura of His communion with His loved ones there in love. Look steadfastly upon the sight, for it is not seen so well but rarely, and I will try to enable you to penetrate some of the details therein."

I felt him intensifying his energizing upon me, and strove to raise myself to meet his endeavours. Success did not come, however, for this was beyond me, as I soon found out. All I could see, more than I have told you, were some vague shapes of beauty moving in the midst of the crimson, fiery glory; no more. So I besought him again, rather piteously as I fear, to suffer me to turn away. And this he did. But I could no more thereafter. I had no heart for anything else. All seemed very pallid as matched against what I had beheld; and I was rather sick at heart awhile that I

---

[29] This is fascinating. Many know of the so called Akashic Records, and some have even communicated about Halls of these Records, but I was not really aware that these records were held in many different locations, and in locations separated by spiritual advancement level, but on the other hand, I was aware that the memories of a particular individual cannot be read by one less advanced. So it makes complete sense that they exist in different locations. G.J.C.

might not go yonder, and be as they must be who endure so much beauty and yet enjoy to live. By and by I recovered and, when he had come forth from the Sanctuary again, in normal guise and robe, I could so far as to speak to him in words of thanks for his very large bounty in giving to such as I what he had given.

Now, what may I tell you more of the doings upon that lofty perch? For you will keep in your mind that only a little of our life and actions here are you able to understand, and that only in part. So that I have to choose very carefully what items I show you; which are such that in some degree I may reproduce in your mind and earth phrasing. One more I think I may try.

A Colony with a Problem.

When the larger visions were ended, we stayed awhile up there upon the roof, and looked upon the country round about us. I noticed, some distance away towards the Ninth Sphere, a large lake bordered with forested land and, here and there, an island, with buildings nestling among trees or peeping above them. Also in the forest ashore was there, now here and now there, a turret to be seen. I asked my guide what colony was that; for a colony it seemed to be, it hung together so well, and seemed one settlement.

He told me that a long time ago a difficulty arose in dealing with those who arrived in this sphere from other regions, who had not yet progressed in all directions as in some of the branches of heavenly science.—I am not satisfied with that; I will try to make it more clear.

There are some who progress evenly in all the faculties which are theirs; but others do not develop all their faculties equally all along their way of progress. These, none the less, are very highly developed spirits, and come to the Tenth Sphere in due course. But had they developed their neglected powers in the same proportion as the others, they would have arrived here much earlier.

Moreover, arrived here, they are at just such an altitude that what served in spheres behind them will serve no more in future. They must henceforth become more equalized in their faculties, and so of more equal balance.

The problem which gave rise to the establishment of that

Life Beyond the Veil

settlement was no other than this. And there they abide doing their work of help to others, and self-training the while. You may wonder wherein is the difficulty. If you do so wonder, that is by reason of the much more complex perfection of the conditions here prevailing than is the case with you.

It arises from the fact that these people are really of the Tenth Sphere in some portions of their character, and of perhaps the Eleventh or Twelfth in other portions. And the difficulty is this: They are in some ways too large in power and personality for their present environment, and yet unable to proceed into the next sphere, where their inferior parts would suffer damage, and catastrophe would ensue which would probably throw them backward many spheres behind, where they would be as ill at ease as ever.

Now, have I made their case clear? If you lift a fish out of the denser water into the rarer air it will have disaster. If you take a mammal from the forest, and plunge him into water, he will die also of the denser element. An amphibian is able to live if he has both water and dry land. But place him altogether on dry land, and he will sicken. Put him altogether in water, and he will sicken likewise.

Now, these of whom I have been telling you are not quite like any of these, yet the analogy will suffice to help you to understand their case. For them to be here is like a bird caged. For them to penetrate higher would be like a moth flying into a flame.

And how is their case dealt with?

They are there to deal with it themselves. I believe they are only in the course of finding the best solution to the problem. When they have done so they will have rendered a service to this sphere which will be carefully recorded for future use. This is continually happening in various branches of study. I think they at present have been able to classify themselves according to their leading traits, and are working on a kind of reciprocal system. Each class endeavours to foster in the others that virtue and power which it has and they lack. So does each, and there is a very complicated system of communal education, which is too intricate even for those who dwell in the Highlands to analyze. But something will come of it which will, when finally ripe to be given forth, add to the power and influence of this region, and that, I think, in some very large measure.

Thus it is that mutual service is rendered; and the royal delight of progress is to help others forward in the way, as we go. Is that not so, my friend and ward?

And so, my blessing, and Good-night. †

Chapter 8

Come Ye Blessed and Inherit

Zabdiel's mission to Fifth Sphere—The Capital City of Sphere Five—Zabdiel's test of the faithful women—The constitution of Sphere Five—The Sixth Sphere—The Initiation in the Sanctuary—Back in the Tenth Sphere—The Temple of the Holy Mount—The King of kings—The Power and the Glory—Zabdiel's farewell.

Monday, December 29, 1913.

Of other things which I saw there I speak not now. It is easier to describe in your earth language the scenes and people and the doings of them which are of those spheres nearer to that of earth. But the higher you go the more difficulty comes in between, and this sphere is somewhat exalted comparatively; and this that I have but just written is of the Highlands of this sphere. So, as before I told you, I am but able to give a very foreshortened and inadequate view of this land and its glories. So let me to matters of more immediate importance to you, and no less helpful.

Zabdiel's Mission to the Fifth Sphere.

I come to a time when I was asked by the Chief Angel Lord of this Tenth Sphere to take my journeyings into the Fifth Sphere for a special purpose, which I will now explain.

I was to go to the Capital City of that region and, presenting myself to the Chief, to inquire of the reason for which I had come there. This he would tell me, having already received word of my coming. Nor was I to go alone, but with me went three companions for my company.

When we arrived at our destination I found the City very easily, inasmuch as I had known it in that time I was a sojourner in that sphere. But how different it appeared now to me after this long time and my many experiences. Imagine it friend. This was the first time I had come here since my advancement from that estate into the Sixth Sphere; and through this and the others I had worked my upward way until the Tenth was reached. Then, after all these stages, and each with its busy life and many incidents to change and develop me, I come back to this sphere wherein, moreover, I had not stayed so long as in any of the others. It was strange, but very familiar, even to detail. The strangeness lay in that when I had first come here from the Fourth Sphere, the glory of it had seemed too great for my apprehension. It dazzled me. But now my eyes had labour to conform to its dimness and want of light.

As we passed through the spheres intervening we conditioned ourselves to each, but went swiftly. When we reached the confines of the Fifth, however, we descended and went on foot slowly from the higher into the lower lands, in order that we might grow into its condition by little and by little. For we should, perhaps, be here for some time, and so would the better be able to endure, and do what work was ours to do.

It was interesting, as an experience, that descent from the mountainous country into the lowlands. There was, as we went down, a continual dimness increasing ever, and yet we were continually accustoming our eyes and bodies to its condition. The sensation was strange and not unpleasant; and to me it was quite new at that time. It showed me the wonderful wisdom which is throughout all and every necessary detail of these realms, this co-adjustment between light and less light, as we went from one onward into the other.

If you understand anything of my narration, then try further to imagine what it means to us when we come through those other less-enlightened realms into your own, to speak thus with you as I do now. Then you will not wonder, I think, that at times we find much to do to get into touch with you, and often altogether fail. Could you see things from this side the Veil you would not marvel at this—the marvel is really the other way about.

Now to tell you of the City.

The Capital City of Sphere Five.

It was on the plain near the middle parts of the region over which the Angel Lord ministered to rule it. It had no walls, as most such cities have; but there were the usual series of Watch Towers, and there were some out on the plain standing solitary, and some

Life Beyond the Veil

within the City, here and there, in carefully chosen positions. The House of the Chief stood squarely and solidly at the edge of the City, and had a large gate.

Now I will tell you not as it appeared to us who came from a higher place, but as it is in the eyes of those whose normal environment is that same sphere, the inhabitants, that is, of Sphere Five.

The Great Gate of this Palace is of liquid stone. That is quite literally to be read. The stone was not solid, but in flux; and the colours of the gate changed from moment to moment, affected both by what went forward within the House, and also by what was going on upon the Plain before it. It also was affected from the Watch Towers on the Plain; but only by those on this side, not by others on the other side of the City, which were in touch with stations on the other sides of the Palace. It was very beautiful to look at, that gateway, massive on either side and blending into the wall of the main structure, solid above the square arch, and changing in beauty as the colours changed. One part only was constant, and that was the great keystone, in the middle above, which always and ever shone red for love.

We passed within and found many roomy chambers about the gateway, in which were recorders who read the messages and influences coming at the Gate, divided them into their own proper groups, and sent them where they should go. They had expected our coming, and two youths were waiting in the roadway beyond the Gate to lead us to the Angel Lord.

We passed down the broad street, whereon went people happy of face, as ever people are hereabout. I simply write it down for you who sometimes and often do not smile for contentment within. For us it is as we should tell you the sky to-day is blue in Egypt in the summertime.

Then we came to the main building within the Palace walls, which was the Chief's own quarters.

We ascended the steps before it and passed beneath a porch (verandah) which ran along its front, and through a door into the Central Hall. It was also square, built with high pillars of liquid stone, like the Gate; and these were also changing continuously in hue, but did not all wear the same tint of colour at any one moment as the Gate did. They were diverse. There were twenty two of them, and each was different. Seldom were two of

Highlands of Heaven

them of the same colour at one time; and this gave a very pleasant aspect to that hall. They were also made to blend together their beauties in the large dome of crystal above, and that was a sight even more lovely, and one you must try to imagine, for it is beyond my power to describe.

We were bidden to rest within this hall, and lay on couches near the walls to watch the play of colour. As we did so the effect seemed to invade us and give us a peace and ease which made us feel quite homely at last in this old-new environment.

Presently we saw a light flash out of one of the corridors which gave on to the Hall. And then the Chief came to us and bowed and took my hand, and saluted me very kindly. He was of the Seventh Sphere, and conditioned to the Fifth, as is necessary to rule it.

He was very kind, and did all he could in love to enable us in every way; and then we went to the Presence Room, where was his Chair of Estate, in which he sat me, with my companions about me, and himself nearby.

Word was given, and a company of women came into the Hall, and greeted us with courtesy. And then the Chief expounded the nature of my visit to me and to my companions, while the women stood before us in their pretty white and blue robes; but their jewels they had left behind, for this occasion. Yet they were very sweet in their simplicity of attire, which was, moreover, becoming to them in the demure demeanour which was upon them in the company of us who were some few spheres removed from them.

It amused me much, and so I asked that he would permit me awhile before he continued. So, descending to the floor, I went and blessed each one, my hand upon the head of each in turn, and added kindly words. Whereupon their shyness was gone and they looked up and smiled at us, and were altogether at their ease.

Now, of the audience which ensued I will tell you when next you sit with me. I have been tied up telling what I had to tell, that you might understand the conditions and customs of these parts. So let us leave it there for this time. I blessed them with words and a touch; and they blessed me with their happy smiles. And so we both were blessed, one of the other. That is the way with us. So let it be with you below. It is better thus than otherwise.

And so also with blessing I leave you now, my ward, for this time, and asking not your thanks for it. For when we bless it is our Father blesses through us, and His blessing, passing through us, leaves somewhat of its benediction in us in its passage. Remember this also, and you shall know that he who blesses his fellow is blessed himself in the doing of it. †

Tuesday, December 30, 1913.

To continue: They stood there before me and I tried to find the reason of my coming, but could not. Then I turned to the Angel Lord for guidance in this matter, and he answered me thus:

"These our sisters are brought here together, who have worked so, in one band, for these three spheres last past. None of them would go before to leave the others behind; but if one should make her progress faster, then she remained to help those who lingered some little, and together they came on until this place was opened to their entry. Now they have progressed to merit their further advancement, if you should judge it fitting so to be done to them. They await your wisdom to that end, for they have come to know that, were they too soon to go forward into the heaven next ahead, their progress would be the more retarded."

Being thus at length enlightened, it came to me that I too was on my trial. This thing had been withheld from me by my own Ruler in order that, with no premeditation, I should be found face to face with a problem, and my wits be put to hazard in the resolution of it. This added to my joy, for that is the manner with us in these realms, that the harder the task the greater the pleasure, knowing our Leader's confidence that we are able if we will.

Zabdiel's Test of the Faithful Women.

So I gave it some thought, and rapidly, and this is how I considered it. There were in all fifteen of these faithful, loving souls, who had so come their long road together. So I divided them by three, and sent five each way into the City. I bade them each bring me a little child, one to each party of five, — and the child should tell me the lesson which they should impart to him, as

Highlands of Heaven

being what most he should have needed to know.

By and by they returned, and with them were three sunny little children. Two were boys and one girl.

Now, they came in nearly together, but not quite. By this I knew they had not met with one another by the way, or they would have joined forces, and not parted again, for their love together was very great. So I bade them stand the children before me, and to the first boy I said, "Now, little one, tell me what lesson you have learned from these kind ladies."

To which he replied very nicely, "If it please you, bright sir, I came here without knowing God's earth, for my mother gave up my spirit into the heavenly land before she gave my body to earth. These lady-sisters, therefore, instructed me, on the way, that I must know that God's earth is the cradle of these brighter spheres. In it are little boys fostered by much rocking to and fro; and no peace is known, as we know it here, until the earth is left behind. Nevertheless, it is of the same Kingdom of our Father's Love, and we must pray for those who are being rocked about unkindly, and for those who rock them too hard."

And then he added, in perplexity at receiving this one last injunction, "But, my lord, this we do always, for it is a part of our school lessons so to do."

Yes it was a very good lesson, I told him, and one which would bear enforcement at other lips than those of his own teachers; and he was a good boy to have given his answer so well.

Then I called the other little mite, and he came to my feet and touched them with his soft little hand and, looking up to me very sweetly, he said, "May it please you, kindly-looking sir—" But at this I could forbear no longer. So I stooped down, and caught him up to my lap, and kissed him, tearfully for the joy of love, and he gazing at me in submissive wonder and pleasure mingled. Then I told him to proceed, and he replied he could not with ease and perfection were I not pleased to set him down on the steps again. This I did, I wondering now, and he continued.

He laid his hand again upon my foot exposed from beneath my robe, and said very solemnly, taking up exactly where I had broken him off so short, "that the feet of an angel are beautiful to the sight and to the touch,—to the sight, because the angel is good, not of head and heart alone, but in the way he goes on the service of our Father; to the touch, for they tread softly ever,—softly where men feel their weight in rebuking for wrongdoing, and softly when he takes up in his arms the sorrowful, to bear him away to these brighter lands of comfort and joy. We shall be angels one day, not little boys any more, but big and strong and bright, and having much wisdom. And then we must remember this, for in that day some one of great degree will send us also to earth to learn and teach at one time; for there are many there who will need us as we do not need who came away so soon. Thus the lady-sisters instructed me, sir angel, and I know it is as they have said since I have seen you here."

Now, the love of little children is always so very sweet to me it unsettles me, in a way, and I do admit to you I lowered awhile my head, and looked within the folds of my lap, while my breast uplifted and sank in its almost painful ecstasy. Then I called all three, and they came—very gladly by their faces, but warily by their feet—and knelt one on either side my thighs, and the little girl before my knees. And I blessed them very earnestly and lovingly, and kissed their sweet bended heads of curls, and then sat the lads on the step beside me and, taking the little maid upon my lap, bade her tell me her story.

"May—it—please—you,—sir," she began, and she said each word so carefully separated from its fellows that I laughed right out; for I knew she had omitted the "kind" or "kindly-looking," or other such endearing adjective, fearing further disaster, and wishing, in her maidenly modesty, to avoid all such.

"Young lady," I said to her, "you are more in wisdom than your years or size, and certain to become a very able woman someday, who will govern well where you are set." She looked at me doubtfully, and then round at the company, who were all enjoying this interview in no common measure. So I bade her, speaking softly, to continue. This she also did, as the boy had done, taking up where she had left off, "that girls are God's dams to nurture His lambs in their bosom, but not until they have grown in love and wisdom, as their bodies grow in stature and in beauty. So we must ever keep in mind the motherhood that is in us, for our Father put it there when we slept in our own mother's womb, before our angel awoke us, and brought us away into these blessed Homes. And our motherhood is very sacred from many causes, and the best cause of all is this: that our Saviour, the Christ Lord (here she crossed her little dimpled hands upon her breast and, with fingers interlaced, bowed very reverently, and straightway continued so), was born of a woman, whom He loved, and she loved Him. When I am grown into a woman I will be told of those who have no mothers as we have here, but know no tender love of mother like ours. And then I shall be asked if I would wish to be mother to some of those not borne by me, but needing some such one as I very sorely. Then I must stand up straight and strong, and answer, 'Send me forth of these bright places into those that are more dim; for I am wishful to suffer with them, if I may perchance help and foster those poor little ones; for they are lambs of our good Shepherd Who loves them; and I will love them for His sake, as also for their own.'"

I was much moved by these three answers. Long before they were complete I had come at several points which showed me that these women must go onward, and together, into higher places; for they were worthy.

So I answered them after this fashion. "My sisters, you have well done in this matter; and your scholars have done well for you. I perceive, among other things, that you have learned what is here to be had for the learning, and that you will be of service in the sphere next beyond. But I have learned also that you will do well to go together as previously, for, although you instructed these tiny philosophers each apart from the others, the trend of their answers is the same—love of those in the earth life, and their duty to them. So I see you are of such a concord in purpose that you will be of greater service together than apart."

Then I blessed them and told them they should journey back with us when we should be ready to go shortly.

Now, several points I did not note for their instruction then, but kept them back for our journeying together, when I could expound them at my leisure. One was this: so utterly at one were these fifteen loving souls that, in their several instruction of the children, they had fixed on one phase of duty and service alone. All these three children and, by implication, all those who had come over here from stillbirth, were to be sent back to help those on earth by tending and guarding them. They had altogether lost sight of all the other manifold duties allotted to such as these; and the further fact that but a small proportion of those who come here in the manner they did are ever sent back to do mission work on earth, for the reason that the very refinement of their natures fits

Life Beyond the Veil

them for other work the better.

But I will no further now, so bid you God's Love and blessing, and on your own lambs, too, and their own dam. Believe me, my brother and ward, those of the Kingdom here look with tender eyes on those who keep their sacred charge in love, and fit them the more for this Realm of great love when they come here. Keep this in mind and be glad that it is so, and within the power of every father and mother among you so to do. †

Wednesday, December 31, 1913.

The Constitution of Sphere Five.

Before proceeding further I will describe the City at which these things were done, for the Fifth Sphere, as I know it, has certain points which are peculiar to itself. Most of the spheres, but not all, have one City in Chief; but Sphere Five has three, and there are three Chief Lords who minister there to rule.

The reason of this threefold dominion is found in that this Sphere stands at that altitude, which having attained, a choice has to be made as to the particular way to be followed thereafter. It is a kind of sorting-room, as one should say, wherein are the inhabitants, in the course of their sojourn there, classified into their proper groups, and proceed onward in that special branch of service for which they most properly are fitted.[30]

These three Cities stand each near the borderland of a very large flat continent, and a line drawn through them would form an equilateral triangle. For this reason the broad roads of each City spread out from the largest square, where stands the House, fanlike, through the City and onward in right lines across the open country. These communicate with the other two Chief Cities and the settlements of the plain. But in the middle of the triangle there is a Temple of Worship and Offering, which stands within a large

---

[30] This is very similar to the concept set out in the Padgett Messages, but found nowhere else, that there are in essence two major spiritual paths, that of the natural love, and that of the Divine Love path. If a spirit reaches the sixth (12 here) Sphere, it is said he must return to Sphere 3 (could be Sphere 5 here?) to take up the other path if he wishes to go beyond that Sixth Sphere. G.J.C.

circular glade in the midst of a forest. With this Temple all the roads are linked up by other cross-roads, and here, at certain times and seasons, come deputies from the Three Cities and settlements under their charge, to combine their worship of God.

Thousands, and tens of thousands, come at one time from all quarters of that sphere, and it is a very wonderful sight to see. They come in parties, and meet together in the glade, which is a large plain of grassland. There they mingle together, and all the different colours of that sphere, mingling also, make a pretty show to behold.

But lovelier than these is the sense of unity in diversity. Some are beginning to progress onward in one direction, and some in another; but over, in and throughout that vast assembly the one vibrant note of deep love pulsates; and all know that this is enduring, and, whatever be their future destination, can enable them to come at one another in whatever part of God's large domain they be forever. So there is no foreboding of coming separation. We know not any such here. For where love is what you know as separation, and its sorrow, cannot come. Even on the earth this would be so now had not man sinned, and so gone away from the right path of development. It will be hard for them to regain this now; but it is possible, for the faculty remains, if it sleep unawakened, except in very few.

Into the Sixth Sphere.

Now we must away to the next stage of my journeyings, when I should take my enlarged company into the Sixth Sphere, and there deliver the women to the Chief of that land.

Arrived there we were met, some way from the Capital City, by a company of welcome. For I had sent the message of our coming from the highlands of the borderland of the Fifth Sphere. They came, and among them were some who had known these women, and the friendship was taken up anew with much joy and many benedictions.

When we had arrived at a town where was to be their home for awhile, the citizens came forth in bright attire, both men and women and some few children. They came along the lane, where we were at that time, to meet us. The trees which grew on either side met overhead in some places and, choosing one such spot, the on-coming company came to a halt and awaited our coming. The scene was very like the inside parts of some cathedral, with leafy roof studded with gems of light; and the people were the choir and worshippers.

They brought garlands of plants and flowers, and beautiful garments and jewels for their new sisters. These they dressed them with, and their less radiant garments melted away and vanished before the new robes proper to the Sphere into which they were now come. Then, each amidst her friends, all happy to welcome and be welcomed as to home, they who had come turned about and struck up a sweet marching air, with instruments of melody, and sang as we went forward towards the town. Here the townspeople thronged the walls and towers and gates, and cried greetings of welcome to add joy to joy already great.

Thus it is that initiates are made to know their welcoming, and, when two or three spheres have been passed through, none fear any longer that strangeness of new scenes and faces shall ever mar their progress onward; for all is love, as they very soon come to know.

The Initiation in the Sanctuary.

We went within the gate and into the town, and came to the Sanctuary. It was a large oval building of very nicely proportioned architecture. The whole, in scheme, was, in significance, that of two circles joined. They symbolized, the one love, and the other knowledge; and the blending of these beneath the central tower within was very nicely and cunningly arranged. Here the light was never still, but ever hanging, like that of the Hall of Pillars I recently described. Only there were two dominant colours here, the one rose-red and the other violet with green and blue in it.

The women were led within, and a large congregation gathered there. Then they were taken to a raised place in the very middle of the Sanctuary, and made to stand there awhile. The keepers of the Sanctuary, with their leader, then made their offerings of praise and, when the worshippers joined with them, a cloud of bright mist gathered from them around the women initiates, and bathed them in the conditions of their new sphere.

When it passed away from them and floated upward,

forming a canopy above, they all stood, in a deep and silent ecstasy, watching the beautiful cloud as it rose and spread out until it covered the space above the other people also. Then came a sound of music, as if it was far away, and yet within the building. It was so sweet and soft, and yet so full of power, that we all felt ourselves to be in the Presence, and bowed in worship, knowing He is ever near.

That music melted away, and yet was with us still; for it seemed to become a part of the cloud of light above us. And, in a way you are not yet able to understand, this is indeed the truth of it. So that cloud of colour and melody of love sank gradually upon us, and was absorbed into our bodies, and made us all one together in the blessedness of holy love.

There was no further Manifestation that they could see at that time. But I, whose faculties have been in longer training, saw what they could not, and knew of those who were present to them unseen; and also from whence the voice came I knew, and the sort of power given in blessing.

But they went away, all very content and very happy together, and the fifteen not the least of them all.

And, Zabdiel, what were you doing all this time? For I suppose you were the highest in degree there, weren't you?

It is not good that I should tell of myself who did but minister in a work of very happy service. The principal of interest were those fifteen. There were three and myself from our own sphere, and none others from any sphere above that one. And to us all the people were very friendly and very kind and loving; and we had much happiness from them by reason of this. Before they would allow their friends to lead them away to their homes those fifteen dear women came back to us, and thanked us, and said very nice words to us in gratitude. We gave them our own in return and promised that we would come again in awhile to inquire of their progress, and perchance give words of counsel. This at their own desire; in which also they showed wisdom rightly named. For it will be helpful to them, I know, and a help not usually given, because not often asked.

So you see the rule here is, as it is with you, as He said, "To those who ask it shall be given." Which word, my brother and good friend, I leave with you to think upon, with my love and good word of benediction.†

Life Beyond the Veil

Friday, January 2, 1913.

Back in the Tenth Sphere.

I would like you now to come back in your mind to my own Sphere, for there are doings there which I will tell you of. By so much as we progress to learn of God and His ways of wisdom, by so much do we come to understand how simple, and yet how complex, are His forces in operation. This is paradox, yet true nevertheless. Simplicity is found in the unity of forces, and the principle on which they are used.

For instance, love strengthens, and less love weakens, in ratio to its lack, every stream of power which comes from the Supreme Father for our use in His service. They who have come so far as to this sphere are able, by what wisdom they have come at, to absorb into their own personalities, to see the trend of things. We see, as we get towards the Unapproachable Light, that all things are tending towards one central principle, and that is Love. We see Love at the Source of all things.

Perplexity is found as from this Source and Centre we proceed outward. Love still runs onward but has, of necessity, to become adapted, by reason of the lower wisdom of the personalities by whom the service of God is done, and is, therefore, not so clearly seen. When these vibrations of spiritual activity, sent forth by innumerable workers in the one great Scheme, reach the cosmos of matter, the perplexity of adaptation and co-ordination is very much increased. If, then, even on earth, His Love may be discerned by those who themselves are loving, in how much greater degree is it manifest to us.

But yet the wisdom we have before us to obtain, if more simple in one sense, is inversely much more intricate, because of the vaster regions over which our view is given to range. As you go from one sphere to another you meet with those whose providence is concerned with ever wider systems of planets and suns and constellations. These you must consult, and from them you must learn ever more widely of the constitution of the Father's widespread realms, and the children of those realms, and His dealings with them, and theirs with Him.

So you will see that we do well to be careful in our stepping forward, that a thoroughness of understanding be had, step by step, for the duties allotted to us become ever wider in their effect, and the consequence of our decisions and actions are filled with greater solemnity, and have responsibility to wider reaches of space and its inhabitants.

I do not deal, however, with other than your own planet in these messages which I have given you, for the time is not ripe by far for such extended knowledge. What we have now in hand, I and my fellow-workers, is to help the people of earth to a higher wisdom in respect to their duty in love one to another, and unitedly to God, and of our ministry of help to such as, in love and humility, are willing to work with us,—we from this side the Veil, and you on earth being our hands and eyes and ears and the words of our mouth to speak forth, as we help you, that men may know themselves as God made them, glorious potentially and, for the time of the season of their earth sojourn, toilers in a world where the light has been permitted to grow dim.

Now let me tell you of those things of which I spoke.

The Temple of the Holy Mount.

On a large plain in this Sphere Ten there is a high mountain which stands sheer up from the grassland and dominates its fellow-mountains like a king on his throne among his courtiers. Here and there about the steep ascent, as viewed from the plain, you see buildings. Some are shrines open to the view on every side; some are sanctuaries in which worship is offered, and on the summit the Temple itself, which is over all, and to which all minister and lead. From this Temple, from time to time, Manifestations of the Presence are given to assemblies gathered on the plain below.

Is this the Temple of which you told me before!

No. That was the Temple of the Capital City. This is the Temple of the Holy Mount. It is higher in degree and of different use. It is set here not so much for worship within, but for the uplifting and strengthening and education of worshippers who assemble on the plain. Keepers and officers there are, who worship within the Temple, but these are very high in degree, and few go in with them until they have progressed some spheres

Life Beyond the Veil

onward, and return on some duty to this Tenth Sphere.

It is a Colony of Powers who are advanced beyond this Tenth in their persons, but who visit this High Place on missions of help and judgment from time to time. And there are always some of them there. The Temple is never left without its complement. But I have not been within, and shall not until I have attained to higher power and sublimity in spheres beyond.

On this plain were gathered a very vast number of people, called there from all parts of this wide Sphere. From some half a mile—as you would say—from the mountain's base they stretched out far across the country, group after group, until they looked like a sea of flowers in gentle movement, their jewels of Order flashing as they moved, and their garments of many hues ever shimmering from one combination of colours into another. High up on the Sacred Mount stood the Temple and, from time to time, they looked that way in expectation.

Presently there emerged upon the roof a company of men whose shining garments told of their high estate. These came and stood upon the porch (verandah) of the Temple, above the chief Gate, and one lifted up his hands and blessed the multitude on the plain. Every word he said was clear and loud to the furthest group. They who stood afar both heard and saw with as great an ease as those who were nearer. Then he told them the purpose of their coming together. It was in order that certain might be presented before them, who shortly should be advanced onward into the Eleventh Sphere, inasmuch as their progress had been judged to warrant their safe journey on that upward way.

Now, none of us knew who these new initiates were to be—whether oneself or one's neighbour. That was left to be told. So we waited, in some sort of silence, the next that should happen. Those on the porch (verandah) stood silent.

The King of Kings.

Then from the Gate of the Temple came forth a Man, clad in simple white, but radiant and very lovely, On His head was a fillet of gold, and gold sandals upon His feet. About His middle was a belt of red which shone and sent forth rays of crimson here and there as He moved forward. In His right hand He carried a golden cup. His left hand was upon His girdle, and near His heart. We knew Him at once, the Son of Man, for none else is like to Him Who, in whatever form or Manifestation seen, ever blends two forces perfectly in Himself: Love and Royalty. There is always a simplicity in His grandeur, and a majesty in His simplicity. Both these you feel come into you and blend with your own life whenever He manifests Himself, as now. And when the Manifestation is over, the blessing so received does not pass from you, but remains a part of you always.

    He stood there beautiful altogether, and sweet beyond my telling—sweet and lovely, and with just a tincture of sacrificing pity, which did but add to the joyful solemnity of His face. That face was a smile itself, but yet He did not smile in act. And in the smile were tears, not of sorrow but of joy to give of His own to others, in love. His whole aspect, and what His form expressed, was so manifold of powers and graces in combination as to make Him One alone among those others who attended Him there, and to set Him above all as King.

    He stood there gazing not at us but beyond us into the realms where we could not follow. And while He stood thus rapt, forth from the Temple, by its several gates, came a long company of attendants, both men and women, whose sublimity was seen in the delicacy of their faces and forms.

    One thing I noted, and will tell you as well as I may. Each of those blessed spirits had a well-defined and powerful character written upon the countenance, and in the gait and actions of each. No two had the same virtues in equal parts and combination. Each was a very high Angel in degree and authority, but each a personality in himself or herself, and no two alike. And He stood there, and they on either side, and some on the lower ledge before Him. And in Him, both face and form, were united, in sweet blend and communion, the beauties and qualities and powers of them all. In Him you could see each quality of theirs distinct, yet all blended together. Yes, He was Alone, and His Aloneness lent added majesty to His appearing.

    Now, think of that scene, and I will tell you more to-morrow, if you find opportunity for my company. Blessing and glory and beauty are where He is, my dear friend and ward, as I have seen, not once nor twice, but many times since I left the earth life. Blessing He brings and leaves with His brethren. Glory is about Him and links Him with the Throne in the High Places of the

Heavens of God. Beauty sits upon Him as a robe of light.

And He is with you also, as with us. He comes not in figure but in fact, into the dim earth plane, and brings there also His Blessing and Glory and Beauty. But there they are unseen, except in part and by a few,—unseen by reason of the dark cloud of sin about the world, as we see it, and lack of faith to look, believing. Still, He is with you. Open your heart to Him and you, as we do, shall have what He brings to give you. †

Saturday, January 3, 1914.

The Power and the Glory.

Awhile He stood in rapture, silent, still and beautiful altogether to look upon. Meanwhile, in the throng of bright ones about Him a movement began. Slowly, and with no haste, the multitude rose into the air, and took shape until there was an oval of light round behind and on both sides of Him. Those in rear were higher than His head, and those in front were lower than His feet. So a frame was made and, as it took shape, their brightness increased until we scarce discerned the forms of them by reason of the brightness of their glory. They shone golden about Him, but He was more radiant still than all the others, as they stood still now, and shining. Only before His feet was there no arc of light, but a breach was made, so that the oval was not complete but gapped at its lowest part.

Then He moved. His left hand He extended and stretched forth towards us in benediction. With His right hand He tilted the chalice towards us, and from its bowl poured forth a thin stream of many-coloured light which fell upon the rock before Him and flowed down the face of the mountain towards the plain. And as it flowed it increased in volume, until it began to lap over the plain towards us, still expanding. It reached us a broad river of light; and in it were seen colours in all their hues from deep purple to pale lilac, from deep red to faint pink, from orange-brown to gold. And all these mingled, here and there, in streams of green or other composite hue.

So it came to us, and among us, as we stood there wondering both at the thing done and all the beauty of it. Now it swept onward until it had covered all the ground on which stood

Highlands of Heaven

that vast multitude of people. But they did not stand in the liquid lake, for it did not rise upon their feet, but formed a sea beneath them, and they stood upon it. Nor could the eye penetrate to see the grassland upon which it rested as upon a sea-bed. It seemed to lie there beneath us very deep, a sea of liquid glass, rainbow-tinted, and upon that sea we stood as on firm ground. Yet it was all in motion, here and there in little waves, and here and there in rivulets of red or blue or other colour, flowing among us underfoot, very strange and very pretty to see.

But in awhile it was noticed that it did not serve everyone equally. There was one here, and another at some little distance, and this repeated throughout the throng, who became conscious of a change in them; and this made them to be silent and in very deep meditation. This change also soon became apparent to their near neighbours. For this is what they saw: the flood of light about him who was thus changed ran yellow-gold, and lapped first his ankles, and then, rising like a pillar of liquid glass, all radiant, and bathed his knees, and then still rose until it was about him a pillar of light, and he in the midst of a golden radiance. Then upon his head, in place of jewel, or chaplet, or whatever he wore, there appeared eleven stars. These also were of gold, but of a brilliance greater than the stream, as if it had become concentrated into eleven jewelled stars to crown the chosen one. On each of those so dealt with that fillet of stars rested upon his head near his forehead, and clasped his head on each side behind his ears. Thus it rested, and shone, making the wearer more beautiful, for the light seemed to invade his countenance and all his body, and uplift him above his fellows.

Then the Son of Man tilted back the cup, and the stream ceased to flow. And the rock became visible once again, where before it had been hidden by the river of light falling. Presently the grassland about the multitude began also to be seen, and at last all the sea of colours had melted away, and we stood on the plain as afore we had done.

Only there remained those who had become enveloped. They were enveloped now no more. But they were changed for sure, and would never be as they had been ever again. Their countenances had become of more ethereal appearance, their bodies also, and their robes were of a brighter hue than those of their fellows, and of another colour. Also the eleven stars

Life Beyond the Veil

remained to crown them with their light. Only the pillar of radiance was no more about them to envelop them.

Now another man came forth of the Temple on the Holy Mount, and cried, with a very strong voice of great sweetness, that those who had the stars should come forth of the crowd and stand before the Mount of Blessing. So they came forth, and I among them —for I was one of those so called—and we stood before the Mountain-foot, and before Him Who stood aloft before the Temple.

While we stood there He spoke to us in this way, "You have well done, my children very much beloved, in what duty has been given into your hands to do. Not perfectly have you served the Father and Me; but as you were able so you did your work. I ask no more than you do after this manner in the wider sphere of service into which now I call you. Come up to Me, therefore, My beloved, and I will show you the path into that higher place where your houses await you all ready, and many friends to welcome you whom you will find there. Come up to Me."

Then we saw that before us arose a broad stairway whose bottom rested on the plain just before us, and the top at His feet, far above upon the Mountain-top. So we all went up that long high flight of steps, and we were in number many thousands. Yet when we were well above the plain and I turned to wave my hand in loving farewell to my group of companions who stood looking after us among the multitude below, it seemed that no less number remained than had come there to the meeting. So great was that assembly.

When we were all come upon the platform before the Temple He spoke good words of cheer and blessing to those who remained on the plain. If any had been in sorrow that they too were not called along with us, no trace remained upon their faces as I looked upon them then. In the Presence of their Saviour Lord none could sorrow, but only rejoice in His great love and the benediction of His Presence.

Then upon the stairway certain angels descended from the place where we now were, and stood upon the steps, from the topmost until half-way down, or thereabouts. They, being assembled, raised an anthem of Thanksgiving, praising God in High Heavens of His Glory. On the plain the multitude responded alternately with those on the stairway. So they sank, and made an end. The choristers once again ascended, and stood with us above. The stairway now had gone away—how I do not know. It was not to be seen there anymore. He raised His hands and blessed them, they keeping silence with bowed heads below. So He turned and went within the Temple, and we followed after Him.

Zabdiel's Farewell

And now, my friend and brother and my ward, I do not say farewell in parting, for I am ever with you to help, to hear and to answer. Count me always nearby, for, although my home in proper is far away, as men would reckon far and near, yet, in a way we know to use, I am ever nearby you, in touch with you, in what you think, and in what you will, and in what you do. For of these things I have, from time to time, to give account on your behalf. Therefore, if I have been anything to you of friend and helper, remember me in this, that in my reckoning I may have joy of you, as you, if faithful, shall have joy of yourself. Remember the Angels of the Seven Churches, and deal well with me, my ward. Remember, moreover, that one day you also, as I now, will have a charge to keep, and lead, and watch and help, and to answer for his life and how he uses it.

And now my blessing. It may be I shall find means and permission to speak with you again as I have done in these messages. It may be in this way, or it may be in ways plainer even than this. I do not say. Much rests with you in this. But, whatever betides, be strong and patient and in sweet simplicity, with humility, and in prayer.

God bless you, my dear ward. I lack the will to bring this to an end. But so it must be.

Remember, I am ever near you in the Master's Name and Service. Amen. †

Recommended Reading

Over a 15 year period I have discovered a great number of extremely valuable revelations from spirit. Anyone who decides to research spirit communications will discover there are literally hundreds of these, if not thousands. And there can be substantial differences between some of them. There are good reasons for this.

As a trivial example, accepting that humans do not change on passing through death, and accepting that there are literally thousands of opinions on life after death on this side of the veil, it's very clear that you need to be sure that you are reading the words of spirits who are honestly communicating what they have personally experienced, and are not speculating on things they have not experienced, but which are based on what they believe.

In the series to hand, Rev. George Vale Owen was very fortunate to have his mother on the other side, someone whom he could trust, and indeed her communications are always absolutely limited to that which she knows of. She then found others to come, of higher estate, and hence he was able to reach more advanced spirit beings.

The recommendations I make here are in similar vein to The Life beyond the Veil. None of course are identical, each has unique Truths to share, and some are undoubtedly more valuable than others. Some are certainly far more advanced in their teachings. All however can be obtained at low cost as Kindle eBooks and many as free pdfs.

The Padgett Messages.

These messages were received at the same time as The Life beyond the Veil, (TLBTV) but have remained in obscurity for many years, partially because they were only published from 1941 on, and took over 30 years to publish the fourth and last volume. These started similarly to TLBTV in that James Padgett sought to communicate with his deceased wife. His wife and his grandmother started the messages to later have higher spirits add their input. These were orchestrated by Jesus and his apostles and are typically of a more religious nature than TLBTV. However they

Highlands of Heaven

also have significant details on life after death, and in particular the structure of the heavens, and the spiritual paths that are available. Most valuable of all is the careful explanation about what it means to be reborn of spirit, and how precisely to achieve that. This is experiential, not intellectual. You do not become reborn of spirit by learning anything. The messages are contained in four volumes, entitled "True Gospel revealed Anew by Jesus" and can be found on the new-birth.net website.

The Judas Messages.

In 2001 a follower of the Padgett Messages started to receive messages from Judas Iscariot. Although not completed, these have a great deal on information on the life of Jesus as well as a number of spiritual topics. The book refers to the Padgett Messages and can be considered a progression of them. The book is entitled "Judas of Kerioth" and can be found on the new-birth.net website.

Trilogy by Robert James Lees.

Robert James Lees completed three volumes, and these have some unique information. In these three volumes we follow a single spirit in his progression, and as a result they span 40 years. The volumes are: "Through the Mists" (1898), "The Life Elysian" (1905) and "The Gate of Heaven" (1931). The very title of this last book confirms the information in both the Padgett Messages and The Urantia Book that the heaven Jesus was talking about is not where spirits initially find themselves. The volumes can be found on the new-birth.net website.

Anthony Borgia and Monsignor Robert Hugh Benson.

Monsignor Robert Hugh Benson was first ordained as a Church of England cleric but converted to Catholicism and wrote many books. He was devastated to discover almost all his dogma was without any basis and set about communicating with Anthony Borgia who he had known as a child.

These books are some of the most detailed accounts of life after death. They are literally packed full of facts and remain probably the most informative available. Although the Monsignor had a lot to say about religious matters, he largely kept these comments to two of the six books. The books of a religious nature are: "Facts" (1946) and "More Light" (1947). The books covering the facts of life after death are: "Life in the World Unseen" (1954), "More about life in the World Unseen" (1956), "Heaven and Earth" (1948) and "Here and Hereafter" (1959). These volumes can be found on the new-birth.net website.

Other Books.

There are a number of other valuable books on life after death that I have summarized on this web page:

http://new-birth.net/other-stuff/books-we-love/books-on-life-after-death/

This page includes a very small book I wrote which can be considered a short summary of what we know about life after death. It is entitled: "Getting the Hell Out of Here."

Geoff Cutler. Sydney, Australia.

Printed in Great Britain
by Amazon